The Community of the Book

A Directory of Organizations and Programs

P9-DEC-937

Third Edition

Compiled by Maurvene D. Williams

Edited and with an Introduction by
John Y. Cole
Director, The Center for the Book

Library of Congress
Washington
1993

Library of Congress Cataloging-in-Publication Data

Williams, Maurvene D.
    The community of the book: a directory of organizations and
programs/compiled by Maurvene D. Williams; edited and with an
introduction by John Y. Cole.—3rd ed.
       p.   cm.
    Includes bibliographical references and index.
    ISBN 0-8444-0807-7
—— —— Copy 3 Z663.118. C65   1993
    1. Bibliography—United States—Societies, etc.—Directories.
    2. Book industries and trade—United States—Societies. etc.—Directories.
    3. Books and reading—United States—Societies, etc.—Directories.
    4. Library science—United States—Societies, etc.—Directories.
    5. Literacy—United States—Societies, etc.—Directories.
      I. Cole, John Young, 1940-
      II. Center for the Book.
      III. Title.
Z1008.W55   1993
002'.06'073—dc20   93-37094
                                                  CIP

Contents

Preface

The Center for the Book in the Library of Congress was established by law in 1977 to stimulate public interest in books, reading, and libraries and to encourage the study of books and print culture. It is a small, catalytic office that shares its ideas and themes with a network of more than 25 affiliated state centers and more than 120 organizations that participate in its program as national reading promotion partners. The Center for the Book's projects and publications are supported by tax-deductible contributions from individuals, corporations, and foundations.

The Center for the Book is a source of information about the world of books and a clearinghouse for good ideas about book, reading, and library promotion. This directory serves both functions.

This is the third—and largest—edition of *The Community of the Book: A Directory of Organizations and Programs* (previous editions appeared in 1986 and 1989). It focuses on national organizations and programs in the United States, though many important international organizations are included. The book and reading scenes in several individual states are described in directories produced by state centers for the book, for example, *The California Community of the Book* (1988) and *The Wisconsin Community of the Book: A Directory of Not-for-Profit Organizations and Programs* (1992). Through Metronet in Minneapolis, the Minnesota Center for the Book provides the same information about events throughout Minnesota, and several other state centers publish quarterly or semiannual calendars of events.

The Center for the Book is grateful for the support of its forty corporate sponsors, whose annual contributions made this directory possible. Special thanks go to Maurvene D. Williams, the Center for the Book's program officer, who has compiled this publication. We hope it will be a useful reference book and introduction to book culture in America in the mid-1990s.

John Y. Cole
Director
The Center for the Book

Is There a Community of the Book?

An Introduction

John Y. Cole

Is there a "community of the book?" The Center for the Book in the Library of Congress was established in 1977 on the assumption that such a community exists and that it can be mobilized to keep books and reading central to our personal lives and to the life of our knowledge-based democracy. The Center for the Book's basic mission is to stimulate public awareness of the importance of books, reading, and libraries. It is a national partnership between the Library of Congress and the private sector that includes more than two hundred organizations at the national, state, and local level.

The most important person in the community of the book is the individual reader. Former Librarian of Congress Daniel J. Boorstin, the center's founder, emphasized this point when the center was created:

> As the national library of a great free republic, the Library of Congress has a special duty and a special interest to see that books *do not* go un-read, that they *are* read by people of all ages and conditions . . . . here we shape plans for a grand national effort to make all our people eager, avid, understanding, critical readers.[1]

In "A Nation of Readers," a talk he presented in 1982, Boorstin asserted that our country was built on books and reading and that, at least in the past, America has been a nation of readers.[2] We can be so again, he maintained, if our citizens and institutions made a new commitment to keeping "the culture of the book thriving."[3] In this effort, which is the central mission of the Center for the Book, technology is an ally: "We have a special duty to see that the book is the useful, illuminating servant of all other technologies, and that all other technologies become the effective, illuminating acolytes of the book."[4]

Publisher Samuel S. Vaughan, in his essay "The Community of the Book" in the Winter 1983 issue of *Daedalus*, defined the book community as one that "consists of those for whom the written word, especially as expressed in printed and bound volumes, is of the first importance." Its major inhabitants, according to Vaughan, were authors, editors, publishers, booksellers, librarians, wholesalers, literary agents and literary critics, book reviewers and book journalists, translators, educators, and "not least, though often omitted from full partnership—readers." Vaughan challenged many common assertions about books and publishing, including his own basic assumption:

> It is convenient to think of ourselves as the Community of the Book. But perhaps we are destined to remain a series of separate states, warring

factions, shouting imprecations at each other across borders. . . . I hope not. For we are bound up in common concerns and causes; we do need each other, and for the usual reasons—because we are mutually dependent.[5]

The search for a "book community" in the United States is not new. The story in recent decades is a mixture of solid accomplishments and periods of frustration. It reflects the tenuous nature of alliances among book-minded people, traditional American uncertainty about the proper role of government in culture, and, especially in recent years, the uncertain effects of new technologies on the world of books.[6]

Finding a Common Cause, 1950-77

In 1950 a small group of leading American publishers, including Cass Canfield of Harper & Row, Curtis McGraw from McGraw-Hill, Harold Guinzburg of Viking Press, and Douglas Black of Doubleday and Company, established the American Book Publishers Council (ABPC), a trade association that would extend itself beyond usual business concerns in order to promote books, reading, and libraries. The first discussions between the council's representatives and librarians took place at the 1950 annual conference of the American Library Association (ALA). Postal rates, book distribution, copyright, and reading promotion were early agenda items.[7] The anthology *The Wonderful World of Books* (1952) was a result of the 1951 Conference on Rural Reading, sponsored by the ABPC, the U.S. Department of Agriculture, the ALA, and other organizations. Theodore Waller, the first managing director (1950-53) of the ABPC, and Dan Lacy, who succeeded Waller and guided the council's affairs until he joined McGraw-Hill in 1966, were the key figures in forging these early book world alliances.

Censorship became a topic of mutual concern to publishers and librarians in the early 1950s, when private groups and public officials in various parts of the country made attempts to remove books from sale, to censor textbooks, to distribute lists of "objectionable" books or authors, and to purge libraries. Senator Joseph R. McCarthy's Senate Subcommittee on Investigations, for example, demanded that the overseas information libraries of the State Department be purged of books that presented "pro-Communist" views. In response, in May 1953 the ALA and the ABPC sponsored a conference on the Freedom to Read. Librarian of Congress Luther H. Evans chaired the two-day meeting, which resulted in substantial agreement on principles and soon led to a Freedom to Read Declaration that was adopted by both associations, the American Booksellers Association, the Book Manufacturers' Institute, and the National Council of Teachers of English, and other groups soon added their endorsements.

The Freedom to Read Declaration and related intellectual freedom issues united publishing and library leaders and their organizations and stimulated, in 1954, the creation of the National Book Committee. Declaring itself a citizen-oriented, public interest voice on behalf of books, the book committee urged the "wider distribution and wider use" of books and encouraged greater use and support of libraries, the development of lifelong reading habits, improved access to books, and the freedom to read. Its approximately three hundred members worked together and with the professional book community to "foster a general public understanding of the value of books to the individual and to a democratic society."

The American Book Publishers Council and the American Library Association, the primary sponsors of the National Book Committee, provided the committee with its small, paid professional staff and with office space. Most of its projects were supported by grants from foundations or by government funds. A Commission on the Freedom to Read was established in 1955. In 1958 the book committee inaugurated National Library Week, a year-round promotion and media campaign that encouraged citizen support for libraries, and administered it in collaboration with the ALA for the next sixteen years. In 1960 the committee began administering the National Book Awards, which honored American books of literary merit and their authors. For the next decade the committee initiated and cosponsored, with a wide variety of organizations, useful conferences on topics such as the development of lifelong reading habits, the role of U.S. books abroad, books in the schools, the need for books in both rural areas and inner cities, the need to strengthen school libraries, and the public library in the city. The book committee also guided development of a "Reading Out Loud" educational television series, which was produced by the Westinghouse Broadcasting Company, and sponsored the initial publication of enduring classics such as Nancy Larrick's *A Parent's Guide to Children's Reading* and G. Robert Carlsen's *Books and the Teen-Age Reader*.[8]

The National Book Committee's sponsorship of projects and publications about the role of American book overseas, particularly in Asia and Africa, reflected widespread recognition of the key role that books could play in economic and cultural development. American government officials, publishers, educators, and librarians established several important programs that stimulated book exports, foreign trade, and international exchange; encouraged publishing in developing countries; and promoted books, libraries, and reading around the world. The major efforts were the Informational Media Guaranty Program (IMG) (1948-68), a program which borrowed funds from the U.S. Treasury to enable United States book publishers, as well as producers of other "informational media" such as films and recordings, to sell their materials in countries that were short of hard-currency foreign exchange; Franklin Book Programs, Inc. (1952-79), a nonprofit, private educational corporation initiated by the publishing community and supported by U.S. government information agencies and foundations to "assist developing countries in the creation, production, distribution, and use of books and other educational materials"; and the Government Advisory Committee on Book and Library Programs (1962-77), a panel of publishers, booksellers, and librarians that met with government officials to provide advice about federal book policies and programs.[9]

Unesco (United Nations Educational, Scientifiic, and Cultural Organization) proclaimed the year 1972 as International Book Year in order to "focus the attention of the general public (and of) governments and international and domestic organizations on the role of books and related materials in the lives and affairs of the individual and society." The National Book Committee organized and supported U.S. participation in International Book Year. The year 1972 was a high-water mark in the United States for cooperative organizational efforts on behalf of books and reading. Two years later the National Book Committee was disbanded, in 1977 the Government Advisory Committee on Book and Library Programs was abolished, and in 1979 Franklin Book Programs was formally liquidated. Thus by 1982, when Unesco sponsored a World Congress on Books to assess international progress in promoting books since 1972, several of the key U. S. organizations that had participated in International Book Year were gone.

What had happened to the programs that made the 1960s and early 1970s such a productive period of cooperation in the United States book community? The Informational Media Guaranty Program had been terminated in 1968 when the U.S. Congress, concerned about the large indebtedness to the U.S. Treasury incurred by the IMG program, denied funds to the United States Information Agency for the program's administration. According to publisher Curtis G. Benjamin, the final controversy over the method of funding IMG was only one of a long series of misunderstandings: "to some [IMG] was a government propaganda device, to others it was a subsidy of commercial exporters, and to still others it spelled censorship." Benjamin, writing in 1984, expressed his hope "that a new (and much simplified) IMG-type program will somehow and soon be organized to meet the challenges that are today as critical as they were in the last decades following World War II."[10]

The National Book Committee was formally dissolved on November 15, 1974. Several related problems had become insurmountable. These included inflationary increases in costs, drastically lessened support from the publishing industry, and the committee's inability to raise basic operating funds from sources outside publishing. In December 1972, the committee had lost the funding and support through services in kind it previously had received from the Association of American Publishers (the successor to the American Book Publishers Council); this separation, according to John C. Frantz, the book committee's former executive director, "came at the worst time in the Book Committee's financial affairs." Other problems also plagued the committee, including management difficulties and disagreements among publishers and librarians about the administration of major projects such as the National Book Awards. A fundamental fund-raising difficulty, according to Frantz, was the committee's inability "to overcome its apparently incompatible, not to say schizoid, origins" and reach far enough beyond the library and publishing professions "to achieve a separate, clearly defined identity."[11] In a parting tribute that called attention to "many fine things" that had happened to books and reading because of the National Book Committee, the editors of *Publishers Weekly* ruefully noted that "some day it will have to be reinvented."[12]

Not only did the Government Advisory Committee on Book and Library Programs have advisory and review functions but it also served as a valuable forum for discussing programs of mutual concern to the government and the private sector, for example, international copyright, tariffs on educational books, and overseas distribution of American scientific books. It also supported such Unesco initiatives as the International Book Year. In 1977, however, President Jimmy Carter asked that all "nonessential" government advisory groups be abolished. The State Department, citing the reduced role that books and libraries by then were playing in the programs of the United States Information Agency and the U.S. Agency for International Development and noting an increased private-sector role in international book activity, recommended that the advisory committee be terminated. This recommendation was accepted in April 1977, and the committee was abolished.

By 1977 Franklin Book Programs, Inc., a significant venture in international publishing that used government and private funds, was also struggling for existence. The major reason was rapidly decreasing support from the United States Information Agency, which had helped fund Franklin from its beginning. But Franklin also faced internal financial and management difficulties, particularly in certain overseas field offices. The United States Information Agency, too, had become increasingly particular about which publications it would subsidize, causing controversy and ill will between Franklin representatives and government officials. According to Curtis G. Benjamin, Franklin Books forfeited much of its government support by "refusing to limit its sponsorship to books that were strictly in line with U.S. foreign policy objectives as interpreted by U.S. Information Agency program officers."[13] Franklin had financed its operating costs by its own earnings and by contributions from foundations, corporations, and individuals and through overhead fees from grants and contracts. With government and foundation interest in its activities sharply decreased, in October 1977 Franklin Book's board of directors suspended all operations.

The decision to close the corporation came the next year and liquidation was completed in 1979. Franklin's remaining cash balance and receivables, amounting to less than $10,000, were contributed to the Center for the Book in the Library of Congress.

Leadership changes in publishing and librarianship in the 1960s were one reason why cooperative attitudes began to fade. For example, Dan Lacy, a consistent champion of closer cooperation between publishers and librarians, left the American Book Publishers Council in 1966. Most industry leaders after Lacy did not share his strong belief in the importance of publisher-librarian cooperation. Economic pressures in the late 1960s and early 1970s also had an effect. Publishers raised prices to meet increased costs, and as the rate of inflation increased, librarians looked to resource sharing, networking, and more selective book-buying to stretch their limited acquisitions budgets.

Copyright, however, was the single most important issue in the deterioration of publisher-librarian relations, and it rapidly became the divisive issue. A bill for a proposed revision of the copyright law, introduced in 1965, grew more controversial as a decade of hearings progressed, with a few publishers actually going so far as to conclude that "the photocopy machine in the hands of a librarian is the most serious threat to the survival of the publishing industry."[14] The new Copyright Law of 1976 did not stop disputes about "fair use" or decrease uncertainty about the effects of new technological changes.

According to economist Robert W. Frase, "Wall Street discovered book publishing" in the mid-1960s, mainly because of "well-publicized increases in federal support for education and libraries" during the administration of President Lyndon B. Johnson.[15] Conglomerates such as CBS, MCA, Gulf & Western, the Times-Mirror Corporation, and Xerox gradually entered the industry. The book-publishing business expanded in the 1970s, but the absorption, or in some cases the attempted absorption, of smaller firms by large conglomerates brought forth charges of "undue concentration" from the Authors Guild, which felt that such mergers threatened the "very existence" of the book community. The dispute was aired at congressional hearings held on March 13, 1980, where Senator Howard M. Metzenbaum went a step further and expressed his concern about "greater and greater concentration" in the bookselling business as well.[16]

The growth of publishing and communication conglomerates heightened distrust. The increased size of many publishing firms, for example, was seen by sociologist Lewis Coser as one reason why so many publishers and major editors seemed to be "losing contact with the world of creative intellect." Coser felt that to the extent that publishers and editors were separated from authors by agents and others, they were likely "to let their general cultural responsibilities remain on the back burner, while the front burner is occupied by business considerations and calculations."[17]

If in the 1970s publishing as a profession turned inward toward business considerations, the library profession continued its inward drive toward further specialization and thus fragmentation. The technological revolution, symbolized by the establishment in 1971 of the first computer-based, online cataloging system, captured the attention of librarians and became a dominant force in the profession. Neither publishers nor librarians seemed able to reach very far beyond their own immediate problems or concerns. Since by then government was in a period of retrenchment, at least in terms of support for education and cultural activities, the decade was an inauspicious time for undertaking cooperative endeavors that would enhance the role of the book in the general culture. Several publishers, however, recognized the need. Writing in the April 1977 issue of *Scholarly Publishing*, Herbert S. Bailey, director of the Princeton University Press, explained that although the book community "should be working together for the advancement of scholarship and for the good of society," it seemed instead to be separated "by a system that puts authors and publishers and booksellers and librarians and finally readers in opposition to each other, so that we often offend each other in seeking our individual interests—in copyright, in selecting publications, in making academic appointments, in purchasing, in the prices we charge, [and] in the uses we make of books."[18]

A modest step on behalf of books was taken in the fall of 1977. At the urging of Librarian of Congress Daniel J. Boorstin, Congress created the Center for the Book in the Library of Congress. Boorstin, a historian who became Librarian of Congress in 1975, was eager for the institution to play a more prominent role in the national culture. In an article in *Harper's* written in 1974, before he became Librarian of Congress, he had explained in detail why "the book" was the best "do-it-yourself, energy-free communication device" ever invented.[19] The development of a new national office at the Library of Congress for promoting books was a natural and logical action. Representative Lucien N. Nedzi of Michigan and Senator Howard Cannon of Nevada, the chairman and cochairman of the Joint Committee on the Library, cosponsored the necessary legislation. The center was established by Public Law 95-129, approved on October 13, 1977, in which the U.S. Congress affirmed its belief in "the importance of the printed word and the book" and recognized the need for continued study of the book and the written record as "central to our understanding of ourselves and our world." President Jimmy Carter approved the legislation to indicate his "commitment to scholarly research and the development of public interest in books and reading."[20]

The new law authorized the Center for the Book to use private, tax-deductible contributions to support its program and publications. Thus the new organization was founded as a true partnership between government and the private sector. Its initial planning meetings and programs were supported by two generous private donors: McGraw-Hill, Inc., and Mrs. Charles W. Engelhard. Over a dozen people who had been closely associated with the National Book Committee, the Government Advisory Committee on International Book and Library Programs, and Franklin Book Programs became valuable members of the Center for the Book's first National Advisory Board, and their previous experiences helped shape the center's early programs.

There are important differences, however, between the Center for the Book and its organizational predecessors, and perhaps these differences will help ensure a long life for the center. The creation of the Center for the Book was supported by the U.S. Congress and endorsed by the president. The center has the authority of a government agency and enjoys the prestige of being part of the Library of Congress, a unique and most appropriate home for such an endeavor. But it does not depend on government funding for its program; in fact more than half its total annual budget comes from private contributions from individuals and corporations. Thus the center has a practical, project-oriented character that is tailored to specific activities that outside donors are willing to support. Finally, the center serves as a catalyst, a source of ideas, and a forum but not an administrator of major programs or long-term projects. Its full-time staff has never exceeded four people. Thus, while it is part of a large and prestigious government institution that also happens to be the world's largest library, the Center for the Book itself is small and flexible, two desirable traits in the fragile and always changing community of the book.

Today the Center for the Book is still pursuing the ambitious mission Daniel J. Boorstin advocated sixteen years ago. It uses the prestige and resources of the Library of Congress to stimulate public interest in books, reading, and libraries and to encourage the study of books and print culture. It is catalytic and opportunistic. "Books Give Us Wings" is its slogan, and expanding the audience for books is still its principal goal. Each year approximately forty companies and two hundred individuals make tax-deductible contributions to fund its projects and publications.

The activities of the Center for the Book are aimed both at the general public and at scholars interested in the history of books, of reading, and of book culture.[21] Its program includes reading promotion projects with four national television networks (CBS, ABC Children's Television, NBC, and the Arts & Entertainment Network), symposia, lectures, exhibitions, publications, multimedia projects, and special events that honor anniversaries or individual achievement in the world of books. The center commissions research and hosts individual scholars. One of its major projects in the 1980s, for example, was "Books in Our Future," a three-year study and series of symposia that explored the changing role of books and reading in the electronic age. The results are recorded in *Books in Our Future: Perspectives and Proposals,* a 399-page book published by the Library of Congress in 1987.

Since 1987, the Center for the Book has initiated national reading promotion themes that have been used by organizations throughout America to promote books, reading, and libraries. First Lady Barbara Bush was the honorary chair of "1989—The Year of the Young Reader," a campaign to stimulate the love of reading among young people, and of "1991—The Year of the Lifetime Reader," which used all media to support family reading and literacy projects. With the 1991 campaign, the center inaugurated a partnership program with national organizations that agreed to publicize the theme, use the theme to develop their own projects, or make a financial or "in-kind" contribution to the campaign. National partners were an important ingredient in "Explore New Worlds—READ!," the 1992 campaign. And more than 120 organizations are national reading promotion partners for "Books Change Lives," the center's promotion theme for 1993-94.

The twenty-six state centers for the book are also important participants in each year's national reading promotion campaign. Each state center is a voluntary, statewide coalition that has been created to work with the Center for the Book to promote books and reading and the state's literary heritage. State centers plan and fund their own projects, drawing on help from the state's "community of the book," from author through reader, and from prominent citizens and public officials who serve as honorary advisers. When its application is approved, a state center is granted affiliate status with the Center for the Book for three years. Renewals are for three-year periods.

The high visibility and the national partnership approach of the Center for the Book complement the plans of Librarian of Congress James H. Billington for the future development of the Library of Congress. In his inaugural address in 1987, Dr. Billington expressed his determination to move the Library of Congress "out more broadly," to see that its rich resources are shared more widely with the nation and the world. In order to increase the institution's usefulness and its public visibility, he has involved the Library directly in contemporary issues facing the Congress and the nation, issues such as education, literacy, economic competitiveness, and the future of Eastern Europe and the states that constituted the former Soviet Union. A major focus is on how to use new technologies to share the Library's resources, nationally and internationally.

With congressional approval, Dr. Billington has encouraged the Library of Congress to undertake a new educational role and established a Development Office to raise private funds for educational outreach projects. Thus the Center for the Book is a small pilot project in the Library's effort to link itself more forcefully and effectively to the nation's intellectual, educational, and cultural life. It is pointing the way to what might be possible through closer alliances among the Library, educational and civic organizations, and the private sector.

The Center for the Book's role as a public advocate of books, reading, and libraries also focuses attention on the essential link between books, reading, and democracy. In a speech titled *Books and the World*, published by the Center for the Book in 1988, Librarian Billington vividly described this relationship and its importance:

> It is important to stress the central moral importance of the enterprise of reading itself for the health of our kind of society. The moral imperative of reading arises first of all from the simple fact that our type of democracy has depended on knowledge and grown through books. By their very nature, books foster freedom with dignity. Books do not coerce, they convince. They speak to the active individual who confronts in private the voice of reason; they do not shriek to some passive crowd cowering before the megaphones of public authority. Historically, books have been companions of a responsible democratic citizenry. They provide keys to the dynamism of our past and perhaps to our national competiveness in the future. Books link the record of yesterday with the possibilities of tomorrow.[22]

Notes

1. John Y. Cole, *The Center for the Book in the Library of Congress: The Planning Year* (Washington: Library of Congress, 1978), 5-6.

2. Daniel J. Boorstin, *A Nation of Readers* (Washington: Library of Congress, 1982).

3. Joint Committee on the Library, Congress of the United States, *Books in Our Future: A Report from the Librarian of Congress to the Congress* (Washington, 1984), letter of transmittal.

4. John Y. Cole, *The Center for the Book in the Library of Congress: The Planning Year*, 5-6.

5. Samuel S. Vaughan, "The Community of the Book," *Daedalus* 112 (Winter 1983): 112. For another perspective on "the shared responsibilities of the book community," see Ann Heidbreder Eastman, "Books, Publishing, Libraries in the Information Age," *Library Trends* 33 (Fall 1984) 121-47.

6. In learning about events in the United States book community from the 1950s through the 1980s, the author has profited from discussions with many of the key participants, including Dan Lacy, Theodore Waller, Robert W. Frase, Virginia Mathews, Ann Heidbreder Eastman, and Carol A. Nemeyer.

7. Theodore Waller, "The United States Experience in Promoting Books, Reading, and the International Flow of Information," in John Y. Cole, ed., *The International Flow of Information: A Trans-Pacific Perspective* (Washington: Library of Congress, 1981), 14.

8. Waller, "The United States Experience," 15-16.

9. Curtis G. Benjamin, *U.S. Books Abroad: Neglected Ambassadors* (Washington: Library of Congress, 1984), 17, 24-25, 34-38.

10. Benjamin, *U.S. Books Abroad*, 20-21.

11. John C. Frantz, "A Death in the Family," *American Libraries* 6 (April 1975), 206.

12. Editorial, "We Shall Miss the National Book Committee," *Publishers Weekly*, December 2, 1974, 15.

13. Benjamin, *U.S. Books Abroad*, 26.

14. Jay K. Lucker, "Publishers and Librarians: Reflections of a Research Library Administrator," *Library Quarterly* 54 (January 1984) 50.

15. Robert W. Frase, tape cassette statement to John Y. Cole, October 2, 1985.

16. John Y. Cole, ed., *Responsibilities of the American Book Community* (Washington: Library of Congress, 1981), 24.

17. Lewis A. Coser, "The Private and Public Responsibilities of the American Publisher," in Cole, ed., *Responsibilities of the American Book Community*, 15.

18. Herbert S. Bailey, Jr., "Economics of Publishing in the Humanities," *Scholarly Publishing* 8 (April 1977) 223-24.

19. Daniel J. Boorstin, "A Design for an Anytime, Do-It-Yourself, Energy Free Communication Device," *Harper's*, January 1974, 83-86.

20. 91 Stat. 1151; Library of Congress *Information Bulletin* 36 (October 21, 1977): 717. Boorstin's initiative was reinforced by a 1976 report of a publishers advisory group, chaired by Dan Lacy of McGraw-Hill, which called on the Library of Congress to strengthen its activities "in relation to the role of the book in American culture." See John Y. Cole, ed., *The Library of Congress in Perspective* (New York: Bowker, 1978), 240-42.

21. For a summary of the Center for the Book's activities since its creation, see John Y. Cole, "The U.S.'s Center for the Book: An Alliance Between Public and Private Interests," *Logos: The Professional Journal of the Book World* 3, no. 1 (1992): 34-40.

22. James H. Billington, *Books and the World* (Washington: Library of Congress, 1988), 8.

How to Use This Directory

Maurvene D. Williams

The Community of the Book: A Directory of Organizations and Programs describes organizations and programs that promote books and reading, administer literacy projects, and encourage the study of books, and whose purposes and interests frequently overlap with those of the Center for the Book. The directory focuses on national, international, and regional activities of special interest to the Center for the Book and its partners, but it was compiled with a broader audience in mind. Coverage includes organizations concerned with authors and writing; book arts and production; libraries, reading skills, motivation and promotion of reading, the state of the book industry, books and technology; intellectual freedom; the history of books; and the international role of the book. Collaborative efforts and organizational partnerships receive special emphasis.

The 109 organizations featured in this directory are alphabetically arranged. At the head of each entry is a block of basic information about each organization, which includes the name the organization and acronym; the address with appropriate postal abbreviations, the telephone number, fax number, and any online access information; the name and title of the person to contact for additional information; and the year in which the organization was founded. Beneath this block are four narrative sections: **What/For Whom**, **Examples**, **Publications**, and **Sources of Support**.

What/For Whom presents an overview of the organization, describing what it is, whom it serves, and what it does for them. Descriptions are based largely on materials that were provided by the organizations and programs themselves.

Examples focuses on those projects that illustrate primarily the organizations's reading and book promotion activities. Many of the examples are collaborative projects developed during one of the Center for the Book's national reading promotion campaigns, e.g. 1991's "The Year of the Lifetime Reader" or "Explore New Worlds—READ!" in 1992. Other examples include programs aimed at special audiences, awards, projects in schools, exhibitions, readings by authors, and media projects.

Publications lists examples of the organization's published materials related to books and reading, including journals, magazines, books in print, and other formats.

Sources of Support describes how the organization is funded and other ways it supports its program.

"A Few Other Resources," located after the alphabetical list, describes a number of related publications, projects, and organizations that did not fit into the main list of organizations.

The index covers the introduction, the directory, and "A Few Other Resources." It includes names of organizations, suborganizations, projects, and individuals as well as giving subject access to the information in this volume.

The listing of organizations and programs follows. Cross-references to other organizations are given in the directory by entry number (§).

§1 ACTION

1100 Vermont Avenue, NW
Washington, DC 20525
202-606-5108
Established in 1971

What/For Whom

ACTION is the principal agency in the federal government for administering volunteer service programs. Its mission is to stimulate voluntary citizen participation to address the needs of American communities, particularly those of the poor, the disadvantaged, and the elderly. ACTION operates through nine regional offices. Its programs are authorized by the Domestic Volunteer Service Act of 1973 as amended.

Examples

1) Older American Volunteer Program. The department runs three programs that include literacy training: the Foster Grandparent Program, the Senior Companion Program, and the Retired Senior Volunteer Program. Of these, the Retired Senior Volunteer Program (RSVP) has the largest literacy project. RSVP provides opportunities for retired men and women, aged sixty and over, to serve on a regular basis in a variety of settings throughout their communities. Senior volunteers work part-time and do not receive stipends. They work under the auspices of an established community service organization with funding, support, and technical assistance provided by ACTION and the local community. For further information, call 202-606-4857.

2) Volunteers in Service to America (VISTA). VISTA added literacy training to its program when Congress passed a series of amendments to the legislation in May 1984. To supplement ongoing VISTA literacy activities, Congress appropriated additional funds in 1987 for the establishment of VISTA Literacy Corps. VISTA volunteers work in recruitment, training, and retention of both tutors and students in low income communities with relatively high illiteracy rates. Priority is given to currently unserved or underserved populations. For further information, contact the VISTA Branch Chief at 202-606-4824.

3) Program Demonstration and Development. Through this office, ACTION funds demonstration grants related to volunteerism. The focus is on innovative ways of addressing social problems using volunteers. Demonstration projects that are funded must have the potential for widespread use through replication. Recent grants have supported projects concerned with substance abuse prevention, at-risk youth services, employment programs, literacy projects, and efforts to assist the chronically mentally ill. For more information, call 202-606-4857.

4) ACTION is a member of the National Coalition for Literacy (§75).

Source of Support

Federal government.

§2 African-American Publishers and Booksellers Association (AAPBA)

P.O. Box 730
7524 South Cottage Grove
Chicago, IL 60619
312-651-0700
Haki Madhubuti, *President*
Founded in 1988

What/For Whom

The African-American Publishers and Booksellers Association is a trade organization established to aid in the promotion, distribution, and sale of African-American literature published by its membership. AAPBA also promotes, encourages, celebrates, and highlights the contributions of African-American writers, publishers, and booksellers and has developed a "need to read" campaign that targets African-American young people in the community.

Example

AAPBA holds its annual meeting during the annual convention and trade exhibition of the American Booksellers Association (§7).

Publications

The association newsletter, published twice a year.

Sources of Support

Membership dues.

§3 American Antiquarian Society (AAS)

185 Salisbury Street
Worcester, MA 01609-1634
508-755-5221
E-Mail: BM.AAH@RLG.BITNET
Ellen S. Dunlap, *President*
Established in 1812

What/For Whom

The American Antiquarian Society is a research library that specializes in American history to 1877. The AAS holds approximately two-thirds of the items known to have been printed in this country between 1640 and 1821, as well as the most useful source materials and reference works printed since that period. The collections serve a worldwide community of students, teachers, historians, bibliographers, genealogists, and authors, whose work at the society reaches a broad audience through textbooks, biographies, historical novels, newspapers, periodicals, plays, films, and library programs. In addition, the society's own library staff prepares scholarly publications, for example, a history of printing in America, and the standard work on Paul Revere's engravings. AAS also awards fellowships and sponsors seminars, public lectures, and academic programs.

Example

The Program in the History of the Book in American Culture, established in 1983, is aimed at stimulating research and education in this interdisciplinary field with emphasis on the study of printing and the distribution of printed material in America. The program sponsors scholarly activities, including annual lectures, workshops, conferences, publications, and residential fellowships. It is sponsoring a major collaborative effort, the preparation of a history of the book in American culture. For further information contact John B. Hench, Director of Research and Publication.

Publications

The News-letter of the American Antiquarian Society, issued irregularly; *The Book: The Newsletter of the Program in the History of the Book in America Culture,* three times a year; its *Proceedings,* once a year; and monographs.

Sources of Support

Private support and federal grants.

---

§4 American Association for Adult and Continuing Education (AAACE)

2101 Wilson Boulevard, Suite 925
Arlington, VA 22201
703-522-2234
Fax: 703-522-2250
Drew W. Allbritten, *Executive Director*
Established in 1982

What/For Whom

The American Association for Adult and Continuing Education is a private, nonprofit national service organization for professionals in the fields of adult and continuing education. Activities include conferences, advocacy projects, dissemination of information, and research and staff development and training. AAACE offers programs in literacy, adult basic education, and English as a second language, as well as in adult and continuing education. Staff development and training services focus especially on training teachers how to teach adults to read and think critically.

19

Examples	1) AAACE's Division of State, Local, and Institutional Management contains the National Council of State Directors of Adult Education (NCSDAE), which, through a network of government-funded literacy programs in every state, provides professional classroom instruction to over two million adults in need of basic reading skills. The Division of State, Local, and Institutional Management also includes the Administrators of Adult Education, which provides similar services at the local level.

2) Life Skills Program. The program includes the Commission on Adult Education, which focuses on literacy and English as a second language.

3) AAACE and NCSDAE are members of the National Coalition for Literacy (§75).

4) AAACE is a reading promotion partner of the Center for the Book in the Library of Congress (§32).

Publications   *Online with Adult and Continuing Educators,* a newsletter; two journals, *Adult Learning* and *Adult Education Quarterly;* and a variety of pamphlets and books on current issues in adult and continuing education.

Sources of Support   Membership dues, conferences, publications, and foundation grants.

---

§5   American Association of Retired Persons (AARP)

601 E Street, NW
Washington, DC 20049
202-434-4700
Established in 1958

What/For Whom   The American Association of Retired Persons is the oldest and largest service and advocacy organization of older Americans, representing roughly one-half of all Americans over the age of fifty. Its purpose is to improve the quality of life for older Americans through efforts in such areas as age discrimination, health care, consumer affairs, crime prevention, tax assistance, research on aging, and adult continuing education. AARP legislative specialists lobby for the interests of older Americans at both state and federal levels. Membership is open to anyone aged fifty or older, whether retired or not.

Examples   1) The Institute of Lifetime Learning is the continuing education service of AARP. For the past twenty-five years, the institute has been helping to ensure that the diverse population of older people has the opportunity to learn by fostering a wide range of educational opportunities for them. The institute produces a number of publications and provides other forums for the exchange of information and technical assistance. Current priority areas include: older adult learning theory and its application, school volunteering, literacy, and skills building. Information is also available on college programs designed exclusively for older people, literacy, and high school equivalency programs.

Besides coordinating with other national aging and education organizations to carry out its mission, the institute works with other AARP divisions and departments to address the educational needs and interests of older learners and to mobilize volunteers to become involved in educational activities and programs. For further information, call, Sandy Sweeney, Chief, Special Projects Section at 202-434-6076.

2) AARP is a reading promotion partner of the Center for the Book in the Library of Congress (§32).

Publications

Modern Maturity, a bimonthly magazine; the monthly *AARP News Bulletin*; brochures; and handbooks.

Sources of Support

Membership dues, magazine subscriptions, investments, and sale of advertising.

---

§6 American Book Producers Association (ABPA)

160 Fifth Avenue, Suite 604
New York, NY 10010
212-645-2368
Fax: 212-989-7542
Managing Agent: SKP Associates
Sandra K. Paul, *President*
Established in 1980

What/For Whom

The American Book Producers Association, a professional organization for independent book producers in the United States and Canada is dedicated to maintaining high professional standards in all aspects of the publishing business. Members produce a variety of titles—from concept to bound books—for publication by trade and other publishers. Book producers provide all the services necessary for publication except sales and fulfillment. They work with authors, agents, editors, designers, photographers, illustrators, typesetters, and printers to deliver either fully edited manuscripts (with or without layouts); camera-ready mechanicals; film for a printer; or finished books. Book producers also assist publishers in developing marketing plans.

Example

ABPA sponsors an annual all-day fall seminar, "Book Producing in the 1990's: How the Professionals Make Books Happen," in New York City. The seminar is open to anyone who is interested in learning more about book production.

Sources of Support

Membership dues and seminar registration fees.

---

§7   American Booksellers Association (ABA)

560 White Plains Road
Tarrytown, NY 10591
800-637-0037
914-631-7800
Fax: 914-631-8391
Bernard Rath, *Executive Director*
Established 1900

What/For Whom

The American Booksellers Association's purpose is "to define and strengthen the position of the book retailer in the book distribution chain." Its members are individuals and firms engaged in the retail sale of books in the United States. Association activities include promoting the retail sale of books, fostering sound bookseller-publisher relations, aiding booksellers in the encouragement of reading at all age levels, and representing the interests of booksellers on legal issues, such as First Amendment concerns and alleged unfair trade practices. The ABA also sponsors national conferences as well as educational seminars and workshops on bookselling for its membership. The American Booksellers Book of the Year (ABBY) Award annually honors titles booksellers most enjoyed selling over the year.

Examples

1) The American Booksellers Foundation for Free Expression was established in 1990 to promote the rights of free speech and free expression; to inform and educate booksellers, other members of the book industry, and the public about the deleterious effects of censorship; and to actively promote and protect the free expression of ideas, particularly freedom in the choice of reading materials. The foundation's quarterly newsletter, *Free Expression*, reports on the threats of censorship and the efforts to shield constitutionally protected materials from these threats. Contact Oren Teicher at 914-631-7800, extension 267.

2) Banned Books Week is cosponsored annually each September by the ABA, the American Library Association (§12),

American Society of Journalists and Authors (§14), the Association of American Publishers (§19), and the National Association of College Stores (§70). Its goal is to highlight books that have been banned, thus attracting media attention to threats against the First Amendment and the importance of the freedom to read.

3) The ABA Literacy Council promotes greater bookseller involvement in eliminating literacy. The council disseminates information about literacy efforts for booksellers who are interested in addressing the issues in their own community.

4) Regional bookseller association affiliates are: Intermountain, Mid-Atlantic, Mid-South, Mountains and Plains, New England, New York, Northern California, Pacific Northwest, Southeast, and Upper Midwest. For current information about these affiliates, contact the ABA.

5) ABA is a reading promotion partner of the Center for the Book in the Library of Congress (§32).

Publications

ABA Newswire is a comprehensive weekly newsletter for booksellers that lists forthcoming publicity about books and authors. It contains succinct information about TV and radio appearances, lectures, articles, and book reviews, as well as major advertising and promotional offers. *American Bookseller*, a monthly magazine of news and features of interest to booksellers, includes a section "Books & the Media," providing summaries of current and upcoming movies and television programs that have a connection to books. *The Booksellers' Book of Lists* features annotated, opinionated lists of the best books in thirty-five categories by booksellers who are specialists in the field. The fourth edition of *A Manual on Bookselling: How to Open and Run a Bookstore* was published in 1987.

Sources of Support

Membership dues and trade exhibits.

---

§8 American Council of Learned Societies (ACLS)

228 East 45th Street, 16th Floor
New York, NY 10017-3398
212-697-1505
Fax: 212-949-8058
Stanley N. Katz, *President*
Established in 1919

What/For Whom

The American Council of Learned Societies is a private, non-profit federation of national organizations concerned with the humanities and the humanistic elements of the social sciences. Its more than fifty member organizations are scholarly associations in areas of language, literature, philosophy, religion, history, the arts, law, political science, sociology, and psychology. ACLS promotes the humanities through fellowships, grants-in-aid, and travel and exchange awards to scholars; investigations into the needs of humanistic scholarship; and cooperation both nationally and internationally with other organizations.

Examples

1) The ACLS Elementary and Secondary School Curriculum Project was established in 1992 to create, disseminate, and implement innovative curricular materials and associated pedagogical strategies in the humanities and social sciences for primary and secondary school teachers and students.

2) The ACLS has directed the preparation of several large, vital reference works, the *Dictionary of American Biography*, the *Dictionary of Scientific Biography*, and the *Dictionary of the Middle Ages*. In 1987, ACLS signed a contract with Oxford University Press to produce a major new reference work entitled *American National Biography* (ANB) which will be a successor of the earlier Dictionary of American Biography. Publication of the twenty-volume set is expected in 1995.

Publications

A quarterly newsletter, an annual report, a series of occasional papers, and periodic ad hoc reports.

Sources of Support

Grants from foundations, the National Endowment for the Humanities (§80), and corporations; fees from members and colleges and universities that are associate members.

§9   American Federation of Labor-Congress of Industrial Organizations (AFL-CIO)

815 16th Street, NW
Washington, DC 20006
202-637-5144
Dorothy Shields, *Director, Department of Education*
Established in 1955

What/For Whom

The American Federation of Labor-Congress of Industrial Organizations (AFL-CIO) represents American labor in world affairs through participation in international labor bodies. It coordinates activities such as community services, political education, and voter education. Sometimes referred to as a "union of unions," the AFL-CIO is a voluntary federation of roughly one hundred national and international unions representing thousands of local unions.

The AFL-CIO actively promotes workplace literacy through its own Department of Education's Human Resources Development Institute. The federation is especially concerned with displaced and laid-off workers who are unable to qualify for retraining programs. Thus, it emphasizes literacy and basic education programs linked to retraining and employment.

Examples

1) AFL-CIO/American Library Association (ALA) Joint Committee on Library Service to Labor Groups. The joint committee was established with the American Library Association (§12) to initiate, develop, and foster ways and means of effecting closer cooperation between the library and labor organizations and the larger constituency represented by the labor organizations. It promotes awareness of common interests among librarians and labor educators and encourages wider and more intensive patronage of libraries by members of the labor community and their families. In recent years, the joint committee has published a bibliography for librarians and others to use in building a library collection about labor, as well as bibliographies on workplace health and safety and on women workers. The committee also gives programs and sponsors film and materials exhibits at ALA conferences.

2) In 1981, the ALA established the John Sessions Memorial Award to recognize a library or library system for its significant efforts in working with the labor community. John Sessions was Assistant Director of the AFL-CIO Department of Education and had been very active on the AFL-CIO Joint Committee on Library Service.

3) AFL-CIO is a reading promotion partner of the Center for the Book in the Library of Congress (§32).

Publications

Education Update, a bimonthly prepared by the AFL-CIO Department of Education, reports on labor conferences, workshops, new publications, and other resources; *Worker-Centered Learning: A Union Guide to Workplace Literacy;* and various pamphlets and bibliographies.

Source of Support

Union dues.

§10 American Institute of Graphic Arts (AIGA)

1059 Third Avenue
New York, NY 10021
212-752-0813
Fax: 212-755-6749
Caroline Hightower, *Director*
Established in 1914

What/For Whom

The American Institute of Graphic Arts is a national nonprofit organization of graphic design and graphic arts professionals. It conducts an interrelated program of competitions, exhibitions, publications, professional seminars, education activities, and projects in the public interest in order to promote excellence in the graphic design profession. The AIGA also sponsors a biennial national conference to celebrate American graphic arts. Institute members are involved in the design and production of books, magazines, and periodicals as well as in corporate, environmental, and promotional graphics.

Examples

1) Competition for the annual AIGA Book Show makes acceptance one of the most prestigious awards for book design. Books accepted for the show appear in AIGA's *Graphic Design USA*. In 1992, for the first time, an exhibition of winning books toured the United States and Europe.

2) The AIGA annually awards medals for distinguished achievement in the graphic arts, including book design.

Publications

AIGA Journal of Graphic Design, a quarterly which includes information on trends, professional practices, and individuals in the field, past and present; *Graphic Design USA*, an annual recording the work selected in the year's national competitions for exhibition and the portfolios and essays on the work of the current AIGA medalist and Design Leadership Award winner; *AIGA Membership Directory*; and other professional publications.

Sources of Support

Membership dues, corporate sponsors, subscriptions, sale of publications, and federal grants (for the national conference).

§11   American International Book Development Council (AIBDC)

1319 18th Street, NW
Washington, DC 20036-1802
202-296-6264
Fax: 202-296-5149
William M. Childs, *Executive Director*
Established in 1985

What/For Whom

The American International Book Development Council was established as a division of the Helen Dwight Reid Educational Foundation in response to problems at home and abroad that create and perpetuate a gap between book needs and availability. The council develops and undertakes projects aimed at enhancing book access at home and abroad and facilitates the exchange of information among readers, in particular among students, scholars, educators, and scientists needing a global exchange of ideas on common concerns. In addressing the needs of this literate community, the council works with individuals and groups in the private publishing industry, international library and book donation programs, education institutions, and governmental agencies, as well as regional and worldwide organizations. The council works in twenty-one areas to remove obstacles that impede the flow of published materials to and from the United States. Bibliographic dissemination, acquisition information, copyright, and professional publishing services are all aspects of its activities.

Examples

1) The council has developed a series of guides titled *How to Buy American Books*, a basic, practical approach to the entire U.S. export community for foreign book importers. The guides are based on responses to a questionnaire the council has sent out to 600 firms in book publishing and allied industries. The ones for Latin America and Europe have been released.

2) The council is participating in a project initiated by the Canadian Organization for the Development of Education (CODE), the development and production of *A Directory of American Donated Book Programs.*

3) American Access to Foreign Literature is another major council program which seeks the cooperation of librarians, booksellers, and book importers in the United States to supplement information gathered from foreign book exporters and publishers.

Publications

American Books Abroad—Toward a National Policy; U.S.-Soviet Book Publishing Relations: Cultural Accord or Discord?; American Donated Books Abroad: A Guide to Distributing Organizations; American Donated Books Abroad: The Publisher's Guide to Tax Deduction; and other monographs.

Sources of Support	Contributions from individuals and corporations; grants from nonprofit organizations, foundations, and governmental bodies.

---

§12 American Library Association (ALA)

50 East Huron Street
Chicago, IL 60611
312-280-3217
1-800-545-2433
Fax: 312-280-3224
Peggy Barber, *Associate Executive Director for Communications*
Established in 1876

What/For Whom

The American Library Association is the oldest and largest library association in the world. In addition to librarians, its membership of over fifty thousand includes library educators and researchers, publishers, and the general public. Its members represent all types of libraries: public, school, academic, and special—the libraries that serve governments, businesses, armed services, hospitals, prisons, and other institutions. The ALA's goals include improving library services, promoting reading, promoting the public awareness of libraries, increasing the accessibility of information, protecting the right to read, and monitoring and improving the education of librarians.

Examples

1) The ALA promotes reading and the use of libraries through public service announcements in national media, news articles, posters, publicity guides for librarians, and public relations campaigns, often in close cooperation with other organizations. "Together Is Better . . . Let's Read" is the ALA's national reading program.

2) National Library Week, held in April, is ALA's biggest annual promotion effort. Each year, ALA's Public Information Office selects a theme, prepares promotional television and radio spots, posters, and other materials, and creates a kit for distribution to librarians throughout the United States. Some effort goes toward national publicity, but the great emphasis is on enabling local libraries of all kinds to enlist local support in promoting libraries and library use. A special reading promotion activity featured during the week is "Night of a Thousand Stars/Great American Read Aloud."

3) National Library Card Sign-up Campaign. In 1987, the ALA and the National Commission on Libraries and Information Science (§76), with the assistance of the U.S. Department of

Education (§104), launched a national campaign to encourage every child in America to have a library card and use it. The campaign has become an annual event.

4) The Office for Intellectual Freedom coordinates ALA programs in the areas of intellectual freedom and censorship. The ALA cosponsors an annual Banned Books Week with the American Booksellers Association (§7), American Society of Journalists and Authors (§14), the Association of American Publishers (§19), and the National Association of College Stores (§70). The ALA also founded the Freedom to Read Foundation (§48), which supplies legal support to librarians and others engaged in First Amendment-related struggles.

5) The ALA Washington office monitors federal legislation regarding libraries. It publishes the *ALA Washington Newsletter.* For additional information, contact the office at 101 Maryland Avenue, NE, Washington, DC 20002; telephone 202-547-4440.

6) The Office for Library Outreach Services trains resource personnel who in turn train others in the library field to develop and conduct literacy programs. The office also administers the Bell Atlantic/ALA Family Literacy Project and the Cargill/ALA Partnership for Family Literacy Program. Management of the National Coalition for Literacy (§75) of which ALA is a member is also a function of this office. For further information, call the director at 800-545-2433.

7) Awards. The Association for Library Service to Children (ALSC) annually awards the Newbery Medal for the year's most distinguished contribution to American literature for children and the Caldecott Medal for the year's most distinguished picture book for children. The Social Responsibilities Round Table honors black authors and illustrators of children's books with the annual Coretta Scott King Book Awards. The Public Library Association sponsors the Advancement of Literacy Award to an American publisher or bookseller for work advancing literacy; and the American Library Trustee Association sponsors the Literacy Award for contributions toward fighting illiteracy. The ALA makes many other awards, most for improvements and progress in librarianship.

8) The Association for Library Collections and Technical Services (ALCTS), formerly the Resources and Technical Service Division, is deeply involved in efforts to study and encourage the preservation of books and other library materials.

9) The ALA administers the Library/Book Fellows program made possible by a grant from the U.S. Information Agency (§105).

10) The ALA is a reading promotion partner of the Center for the Book in the Library of Congress (§32).

Publications	*American Libraries* is a monthly membership magazine that covers the breadth of ALA's interests with news and feature articles. Each of ALA's divisions publishes a journal and many publish newsletters. *Booklist* provides prepublication book reviews for public libraries; *Choice* does the same for college and university libraries. The ALA publishes many books in library management and technical services as well as literacy and censorship. Booklists, many of them pamphlets, are available from ALA. These are selective lists of readings, some arranged by topic, others by audience (adults, young adults, children). Some are not only selective but the result of awards selections. Posters promoting libraries, books, and reading are also available from ALA. Their books catalog and graphics catalog list currently available items.
Sources of Support	Membership fees, endowment income, conference proceeds, and grants from foundations and government agencies.

§13 American Printing History Association (APHA)

P.O. Box 4922, Grand Central Station
New York, NY 10163
212-673-8770
Stephen Crook, *Executive Secretary*
Founded in 1974

What/For Whom	The American Printing History Association is a nonprofit membership organization founded to encourage the study of printing history and its related arts and skills, including calligraphy, typefounding, papermaking, bookbinding, illustration, and publishing. The association has members from throughout the book world, including book collectors, librarians, printers, editors, private press owners, and historians. It sponsors exhibits and conferences and presents annual awards for outstanding contributions to printing history. APHA both coordinates projects in the history of printing and encourages the preservation of the artifacts of the printing trade by museums.
Example	The fall conferences of APHA have each focused on a topic in printing history, such as American newspaper printing, collecting printing history, and the beginning of printing in the United States.
Publications	The *APHA Newsletter*, a bimonthly, covers the full range of APHA's interests including news, listings of lectures and exhibitions, book reviews, and notices of printing equipment for sale. *Printing History* is a semiannual scholarly journal with articles reflecting the broad range of printing and book history, as well as reviews and other features.
Sources of Support	Membership dues, contributions, and sale of publications.

§14 American Society of Journalists and Authors (ASJA)

1501 Broadway, Suite 302
New York, NY 10036
212-997-0947
Fax: 212-768-7414
Alexandra S. E. Cantor, *Executive Director*
Founded in 1948

What/For Whom

The American Society of Journalists and Authors is a nation-wide organization of independent nonfiction writers. The membership consists of more than eight hundred freelance writers of magazine articles, trade books, and many other forms of nonfiction writing. The society presents awards and conducts meetings, seminars, and an annual convention with exhibits. The ASJA offers referral service, for members only, to connect business firms, publishers, and others with writers offering special skills and experience.

Examples

1) Each spring the annual ASJA Writer's Conference brings together writers, publishers, and editors who explore, in panel discussions and workshops, current markets and trends in books, magazines, and other media.

2) The ASJA sponsors the Llewellyn Miller Fund to aid professional writers no longer able to work because of age, disability, or extraordinary professional crisis.

3) The Conscience-in-Media Gold Medal Award and awards for excellence in writing and magazine publishing are presented each year.

4) The ASJA is a cosponsor of the annual Banned Books Week through their "I Read Banned Books" campaign.

Publications

ASJA Newsletter, monthly; a membership directory; and several books on nonfiction writing.

Sources of Support

Membership dues.

§15 American Wholesale Booksellers Association (AWBA)

702 South Michigan Street
South Bend, IN 46601
212-232-8500, extension 23
Michael J. Raymond, *Executive Secretary*
Founded in 1984

What/For Whom

The American Wholesale Booksellers Association, representing book wholesalers throughout the United States and Canada, educates retailers and publishers about the fundamentals of wholesaling in the book industry, develops and advances industry standards, and provides wholesalers with a forum through which industry-wide questions can be addressed. Membership is open to book wholesalers, and to publishers, who may become nonvoting, associate members.

Examples

1) AWBA meets with the Association of American Publishers (§19) annually to discuss issues and concerns affecting wholesalers and trade publishers.

2) AWBA meets regularly with publishers and retailers to address industry concerns. Issues have included: standardization of ISBN use, title abbreviations, market expansion, returns to publishers, and the future of wholesaling.

Publications

Directory and Customer Handbook, an annual and a video that explains the basic reasons for using wholesalers, can be presented to the book industry at workshops, lectures, and schools.

Sources of Support

Membership dues.

§16 Antiquarian Booksellers Association of America (ABAA)

50 Rockefeller Plaza
New York, NY 10020
212-757-9395
Fax: 212-459-0307
Liane Wood-Thomas, *Executive Director*
Founded in 1949

What/For Whom

The Antiquarian Booksellers Association of America was founded to encourage interest in rare books and manuscripts and to maintain the highest standards in the antiquarian book trade in the United States. Its members are dealers in rare and out-of-print books. ABAA promotes exhibitions of books and related materials and offers courses and lectures on subjects of interest to book collectors. The association comments on proposed legislation relevant to its members, maintains relations with other organizations concerned with rare books, and sets guidelines for professional conduct for dealers. It also maintains an Antiquarian Booksellers' Benevolent Fund.

Publications

ABAA Newsletter, a directory of its members, and a pamphlet, *Guidelines for the Antiquarian Booksellers Association of America*, which concerns professional ethics.

Source of Support

Membership fees.

---

§17 Associated Writing Programs (AWP)

Old Dominion University
Norfolk, VA 23529-0079
804-683-3839
Markham Johnson, *Executive Director*
Established in 1967

What/For Whom

The Associated Writing Programs is a national nonprofit organization that fosters literary talent and achievement, advances the craft of writing as primary to a liberal and humane education, and serves the makers and readers of contemporary writing both within the academic community and beyond. The AWP also serves as an advocate of creative writing as an art and works to gain public and private support for literary artists. Its membership of more than seventy-five hundred are writers, students and teachers in writing programs, editors, publishers, and creative and professional writers. The AWP operates a placement service to help writers find jobs and it sponsors workshops, readings, conferences, symposia, and various literary competitions.

Examples

1) The AWP Award Series is a national competition held each year for the publication of outstanding new works of poetry, short fiction, the novel, and creative nonfiction.

2) The AWP's annual conference brings together writers, teachers, publishers, and editors and features readings, addresses, a bookfair, and panels on American letters and pedagogy.

3) Each fall, in coordination with Old Dominion University, the AWP cosponsors a literary festival in Virginia's Tidewater region.

Publications   *AWP Chronicle*, issued six times a year; *The AWP Official Guide to Writing Programs*, a comprehensive guide to creative writing programs; and the *AWP Job List.*

Sources of Support   Membership dues, sale of publications, and contributions.

---

§18 Association for Community-Based Education (ACBE)

1805 Florida Avenue, NW
Washington, DC 20009
202-462-6333
Fax: 202-232-8044
Christofer P. Zachariadis, *Executive Director*
Established in 1976

What/For Whom   The Association for Community-Based Education is a national nonprofit network of member organizations providing alternative education programs linked to the needs, cultures, and traditions of the communities they serve. Community-based organizations offer programs aimed at both individual and community-wide development. They respond to underserved populations by carrying out a range of activities that include economic development, housing rehabilitation, health services, job training, adult literacy, and continuing education programs.

Services to member organizations include minigrants, technical assistance, professional development training, advocacy, informational services, a database and clearinghouse to collect and disseminate information about community-based education and its needs for resources, an awards program, fellowships, scholarships, and an annual conference.

Examples   1) The ACBE is a member of the National Coalition for Literacy (§75).

2) Adult literacy is one of ACBE's major priorities. Its research has focused on describing community-based literacy programs around the country by collecting data on their organization, methods, participants, and impact. In 1989, ACBE conducted the first national survey of these programs. Through its literacy initiative, ACBE acts to strengthen community-based literacy programs, support their achievements, and advocate on their behalf.

Publications   *CBE Report,* a monthly, contains information about national policies and programs, funding opportunities, workshops, conferences, and publications and about successful programs and practices at the local level. The ACBE also publishes technical assistance bulletins, an annual report, an annual membership directory, conference proceedings, and special reports on programs and practices.

Sources of Support   Contributions from private foundations and corporations, membership dues, the sale of publications, and annual conference fees.

---

§19   Association of American Publishers, Inc. (AAP)

220 East 23d Street
New York, NY 10010-4606
212-689-8920
Fax: 212-696-0131

1718 Connecticut Avenue, NW
Washington, DC 20009-1148
202-232-3335
Fax: 202-745-0694

Nicholas A. Veliotes, *President*
Established in 1970

What/For Whom   The Association of American Publishers, Inc., with more than two hundred members located in every region of the United States, is the principal trade association of the book publishing industry. AAP members publish hardcover and paperback books in every field, including general fiction and nonfiction, poetry, children's books, textbooks, Bibles and other religious books, reference works, scientific, medical, technical, professional and scholarly books and journals, and classroom instructional and testing materials. Members of the association also produce computer software and electronic products and services, such as online databases, CD-ROM, and CD-I.

The association's highest priorities are: expanding domestic and foreign markets for American books, journals, and electronic publishing products; promoting the status of publishing in the United States and abroad; defending intellectual freedom at home and the freedom of written expression worldwide; keeping AAP member publishers informed about legislative, regulatory, and policy issues that affect the industry and serving as the industry's voice on these issues; protecting the rights of creators through ongoing efforts in defense of copyright; and offering practical educational programs to assist members in the management of their companies. Services include conferences, statistical surveys, public information, and press relations.

Examples

1) The AAP Reading Initiative, established in 1989, acts as a clearinghouse for information on literature-based reading programs, puts teachers in contact with other teachers who are using a literature-based approach to reading, opens the lines of communication between children's trade book publishers and classroom teachers, and works closely with other professional organizations to ensure that children read widely and well. The "Teachers as Readers" project, an outgrowth of this initiative, has among its group participants the American Library Association (§12), International Reading Association (§61), and the National Council of Teachers of English (§77).

2) The Freedom to Read Committee is concerned with protecting freedoms guaranteed by the First Amendment. It analyzes individual cases of attempted censorship and may take action in the form of legal briefs, testimony before appropriate legislative committees, or public statements and telegrams protesting any attempt to limit freedom of communication. It also sponsors public programs and issues periodic educational reports on censorship. For additional information, contact Richard P. Kleeman, Director, Freedom to Read, in the AAP Washington office.

3) The International Freedom to Publish Committee defends and broadens the freedom of written communication internationally. It monitors human rights issues and offers moral support and practical assistance to publishers and authors who are denied basic freedoms. Recent examples include letters sent to Fidel Castro protesting the arrests of members of the Movimiento Armonia and the imprisonment of writers Ynadamiro Restano and Maria Elena Aparicio; and to Egyptian government officials on behalf of writer Alaa Hamid, his publisher, and his distributor, who were tried and sentenced to prison for blasphemy.

4) The AAP is a cosponsor of the annual Banned Books Week.

5) The AAP is a reading promotion partner of the Center for the Book in the Library of Congress (§32).

Publications

AAP Monthly Report, a news bulletin giving comprehensive coverage of association activities; *AAP Reading Initiative News*, an occasional newsletter; and other items of interest to the industry.

Sources of Support

Membership dues, sale of publications, and proceeds from conferences.

§20 Association of American University Presses, Inc. (AAUP)

584 Broadway, Suite 410
New York, NY 10012-3264
212-941-6610
Fax: 212-941-6618
Peter C. Grenquist, *Executive Director*
Established in 1937

What/For Whom

The AAUP is a cooperative nonprofit organization that promotes the work and influence of university presses, provides cooperative marketing efforts, and helps its presses respond to the changing economy and environment. Its programs, which are primarily designed to help its one hundred member presses market their publications and train their personnel more effectively, include: annual and regional meetings, seminars, workshops, exhibits and statistical programs, and an annual design competition.

Examples

1) The AAUP sponsors several workshops per year, each focusing on a particular area, such as financial management, book design, planning for press growth, advertising techniques, and editing electronic manuscripts.

2) The AAUP is a reading promotion partner of the Center for the Book in the Library of Congress (§32).

Publications

The Exchange, a quarterly newsletter; the annual bibliographies *University Press Books for Public Libraries and for Secondary School Libraries;* their annual directory; and brochures and pamphlets.

Sources of Support

Membership dues, conferences, and publications.

§21 Association of Booksellers for Children (ABC)

4412 Chowan Avenue South
Minneapolis, MN 55410
612-926-6650
Caron Chapman, *Executive Director*
Established in 1985

What/For Whom

The Association of Booksellers for Children is an international organization that offers support and resources to professional booksellers specializing in children's books and encourages quality throughout the children's book industry.

The ABC provides services, studies, and programs for the advancement of children's books; promotes high standards in business methods and ethics; and encourages a fraternal spirit among its members. Members include retail booksellers, who are voting members, and authors, illustrators, publishers, and wholesalers, who are associate members.

Examples

1) ABC's *Bookfair Kit* is a packet of information and sample materials compiled by members who have shared their experiences with school bookfairs, including step-by-step procedures, examples of marketing materials, and some cost factors.

2) Each year, members of ABC select children's books of the previous year for the Children's Booksellers' Choices. The results are listed on bookmarks for members to use.

3) The ABC is a reading promotion partner of the Center for the Book in the Library of Congress (§32).

Publications

Building Blocks, a quarterly newsletter; *Building Blocks Catalog*, a backlist catalog of children's books; an annual membership directory; and other resources to help members promote children's books.

Sources of Support

Membership dues, sale of mailing lists, and contributions.

---

§22   Association of Research Libraries (ARL)

21 Dupont Circle, NW
Washington, DC 20036
202-296-2296
Fax: 202-872-0884
Duane E. Webster, *Executive Director*
Founded in 1932

What/For Whom

The Association of Research Libraries, made up of more than 119 libraries that serve major North American research institutions, identifies and influences forces affecting the future of research libraries in their promotion of scholarly communication. In support of teaching, research, scholarship, and community service, ARL's programs and services promote equitable access to recorded knowledge and effective use of it. Articulating the concerns of research libraries and their institutions, ARL forges coalitions for cooperative action, influences information policy development, and supports innovation and improvement in research library programs.

Examples	1) The Office of Scientific and Academic Publishing (OSAP) was established to identify and influence the forces affecting the production, dissemination, and use of scholarly and scientific information.
	2) The Office of Management Services (OMS) conducts research and provides consulting, information, and training in the management of human and material resources in libraries.
	3) ARL is a reading promotion partner of the Center for the Book in the Library of Congress (§32).
Publications	*ARL: A Bimonthly Newsletter of Research Library Issues and Actions* and other publications.
Sources of Support	Membership dues and grants from the National Endowment for the Humanities (§80).

§23 Authors League of America, Inc., and Authors Guild, Inc.

330 West 42d Street
New York, NY 10036
212-564-8350 (Authors League)
212-563-5904 (Authors Guild)
Julie Tate, Assistant Director

What/For Whom

The Authors League of America, founded in 1912, represents the interests of authors and playwrights regarding copyright, freedom of expression, taxation, and other issues. It consists of two component organizations, the Dramatists Guild and the Authors Guild, Inc.

The Authors Guild, Inc., founded in 1921, is the national society of professional authors, representing over sixtyfive hundred writers of books, poetry, articles, short stories, and other literary works in matters of business and professional interests. The guild and the league conduct several symposia each year at which experts provide information on such subjects of interest as rights of privacy and publicity, libel, wills and estates, taxation, copyright, editors and editing, the art of interviewing, and standards of criticism and book reviewing.

Example

The Authors League represents the interests of authors in the work of the Copyright Office of the Library of Congress (see §64), dealing with library photocopying and other major copyright issues. In addition, the Authors League files amicus curiae briefs on behalf of writers in the Supreme Court and in United States and state appellate courts; testifies before congressional and state legislative committees; and issues public statements on various First Amendment issues, among them secrecy clauses in government contracts and book banning in schools.

Publications

The *Authors Guild Bulletin*, various leaflets, and pamphlets.

Sources of Support

Membership dues from the Dramatists Guild and the Authors Guild and activities fees.

---

§24   The Barbara Bush Foundation for Family Literacy

1002 Wisconsin Avenue, NW
Washington, DC 20007
202-338-2006
Fax: 202-337-6754
Benita Somerfield, Executive Director
Established 1989

What/For Whom

The Barbara Bush Foundation for Family Literacy is a nonprofit volunteer organization that supports the development of family literacy programs. Its aim is to break the intergenerational cycle of illiteracy and establish literacy as a value in every family in America. The foundation identifies family literacy programs that are successful, awards grants to help establish successful family literacy efforts, provides seed money for community planning of interagency family literacy programs, supports training and professional development for teachers, encourages recognition of volunteers, educators, students, and effective programs, and publishes and distributes materials that document effective working programs.

Examples

1) The Barbara Bush Foundation for Family Literacy annually awards an average twelve grants totaling up to $500,000 to public and private programs.

2) The foundation is a reading promotion partner of the Center for the Book in the Library of Congress (§32).

Publications

First Teachers: A Family Literacy Handbook for Parents, Policymakers, and Literacy Providers, published with support from the Association of American Publishers (§19), highlights model family literacy programs. *Barbara Bush's Family Reading Tips*, a pamphlet published in both English and in Spanish, is designed to encourage parents and other caregivers to read to children.

Sources of Support

Corporate and individual donations.

§25 Bibliographical Society of America

P.O. Box 397, Grand Central Station
New York, NY 10163
212-995-9151
Fax: 212-481-9698
Marjory Zaik, Executive Secretary
Established in 1904

What/For Whom

The Bibliographical Society of America promotes bibliographical research and issues a variety of bibliographical publications. It sponsors a short-term fellowship program in bibliography. Specific interests include the history of book production, publication, distribution, collecting, and author bibliography. Membership is open to libraries and individuals interested in bibliographical problems and projects.

Example

The Bibliographical Society holds its annual meeting each January in New York City and cosponsors meetings with other organizations in various parts of the country from time to time.

Publications

The quarterly journal *Papers* and occasional monographs. The society provides editorial supervision of publication of the ongoing *Bibliography of American Literature.*

Sources of Support

Membership dues, foundation grants, and sale of publications.

§26 Book Industry Study Group, Inc. (BISG)

160 Fifth Avenue, Suite 604
New York, NY 10010-7000
212-929-1393
Fax: 212-989-7542
Managing Agent: SKP Associates
Sandra K. Paul, President
Established in 1976

What/For Whom

The purpose of the Book Industry Study Group is to promote and support research in and about the industry. BISG is a voluntary, nonprofit research organization composed of individuals and firms from various sectors of the book industry: publishers, manufacturers, suppliers, wholesalers, retailers, librarians, and others engaged professionally in the development, production, and dissemination of books. The group began when the Book Manufacturers' Institute (§27) brought together publishers, manufacturers, and representatives of trade associations to discuss the need to improve the industry's research capability. Trade and professional associations, such as the American Booksellers Association (§7), American Wholesale Booksellers Association (§15), the Association of American Publishers (§19), and the National Association of College Stores (§70) have joined in this effort to meet the book industry's research and information needs.

Examples

1) BISG's *1991/1992 Consumer Research Study on Book Purchasing* examines the book purchasing habits of sixteen thousand households. It identifies the place of purchase, category of title, price paid, and buyer demographics. It also differentiates purchases of adult and juvenile books.

2) BISG has become the source of bar-coding information for the book industry and offers two booklets on bar coding for books and their cartons (*Machine-readable Coding Guidelines for the U.S. Book Industry and Guidelines for Shipping Container Codes* and *Symbols for the U.S. Book Industry*) and one for scientific and technical journals (*Serial Item Identifier: Bar Code Symbol Implementation Guidelines*).

3) The Book Industry Systems Advisory Committee (BISAC) helps in developing voluntary standardized computer-to-computer communications formats used throughout the industry and in expanding the acceptance of the International Standard Book Number (ISBN) and the Standard Address Number (SAN) within the publishing and bookselling community. The Serials Industry Systems Advisory Committee (SISAC) provides a forum for the serials industry to discuss mutual concerns and problems.

4) BISG and *Publishers Weekly* cosponsor an annual seminar devoted to emerging economic trends in the book industry and other issues of concern such as the First Amendment, returns policies, and education.

Publications

Book Industry Trends, an annual statistical research report used by the industry in business planning and other research reports. *Book Industry Trends 1993* covers the years 1987-93.

Sources of Support

Membership dues and sale of publications.

§27 Book Manufacturers' Institute, Inc. (BMI)

45 William Street, Suite 150
Wellesley, MA 02181-4007
617-239-0103
Fax: 617-239-0106
Stephen P. Snyder, *Executive Vice President*
Established in 1933

What/For Whom

Book Manufacturers' Institute, Inc., is the leading trade association of the book manufacturing industry. Its members manufacture the majority of books published by the U.S. book publishing industry each year. BMI brings together book manufacturers to deal with common concerns and also provides links between book manufacturers and publishers, suppliers, and governmental bodies. BMI conducts studies and seminars, collects statistics, and makes forecasts about the industry's future. Each year BMI conducts one fall conference and a management conference in the spring. BMI also administers an awards program to recognize its members.

Examples

1) Through its affiliation with the Book Industry Study Group (§26), which it helped create, BMI has developed a data information program for the industry.

2) The Government Relations Committee and the Postal Committee of BMI have worked with their counterparts at the Association of American Publishers (§19) to present the positions of their two industries to various governmental and legislative bodies.

3) With the Association of American Publishers and the National Association of State Textbook Administrators, BMI has developed nationally recognized manufacturing standards for textbooks.

4) BMI produced *The Well-Built Book: Art and Technology*, a video presentation which explains the book manufacturing process from pre-press to press to bindery.

Publications

The *BMI Newsletter* and *Who's Who in Book Manufacturing*, an annual membership directory.

Sources of Support

Membership dues and tape and film sales.

§28   Bookbuilders West (BBW)

P.O. Box 7046
San Francisco, CA 94120-9727
415-595-2350
Patricia Brewer, *President*
Founded 1969

What/For Whom

Bookbuilders West is a nonprofit association founded to promote and support book publishing in the thirteen western states. It sponsors a wide variety of education programs designed to inform members about advances in publishing methods and processes or to investigate technological or aesthetic problems and solutions. BBW fosters publishing excellence and public recognition through an annual book show and encourages qualified graphic arts students in western colleges through its annual scholarship and internship programs.

Examples

1) BBW awards one or more scholarships annually to deserving students in graphic arts, editorial, or marketing courses. Summer internship programs attract gifted young people to book publishing in the West.

2) PubForum, a three-day event, features seminars and exhibits from suppliers.

Publications

BBW Newsletter, a bimonthly that features news and events in western book publishing, and *The Directory of Western Book Publishers and Production Services*.

Source of Support

Membership dues.

§29   Cartoonists Across America (CAA)

P.O. Box 670
Lompoc, CA 93438-0670
805-735-5134
Fax: 805-735-7541
Philip Yeh, *Director*
Established in 1985

What/For Whom

Cartoonists Across America is a group of cartoon artists and writers who use creativity, humor, and a variety of graphic styles to demonstrate the importance of reading to the American public and to audiences in foreign countries. Members make appearances on request at schools, community centers, bookstores, city halls, prisons, conventions and conferences, hospitals, corporations, and fund-raising events.

Examples

1) In 1986, Cartoonists Across America began painting large dinosaur murals with the slogan "Read, Avoid Extinction" all across the United States. The organization has painted more than 450 murals in forty-eight states, three Canadian provinces, and European countries in sites from convention centers and malls to museums and schools. During the Bicentennial of the Constitution in 1987, CAA drew a giant cartoon strip to call attention to the issue of literacy and the importance of the U.S. Constitution. Its projects have also included painting city buses and trash haulers to promote reading, recycling, and clean air.

2) Cartoonists Across America is a reading promotion partner of the Center for the Book in the Library of Congress (§32).

Publications

Several cartoon book series to promote literacy for all ages, including the *Frank the Unicorn, Patrick Rabbit,* and *Theo the Dinosaur,* trade paperback books; and other products, such as T-shirts, posters, and bumper stickers with the dinosaurs-for-literacy theme.

Sources of Support

Corporate sponsors and sale of publications and other products.

---

§30 Center for Applied Linguistics (CAL)

1118 22d Street, NW
Washington, DC 20037
202-429-9292
Fax: 202-429-9766
Sara Melendez, *President*
Established in 1959

What/For Whom

The Center for Applied Linguistics is a private, nonprofit resource organization established in 1959 as an autonomous program of the Modern Language Association (§67) and incorporated in 1964 as an independent organization. CAL promotes the application of linguistic findings to practical language problems, conducts research and disseminates information on language and linguistics, generates educational materials illustrating various approaches to literacy, evaluates reading programs and proposed reading tests, including those being considered for statewide adoption, and serves as an intermediary in bringing together people and institutions concerned with language problems.

The center focuses on two program areas: literacy education and work to reduce the (English) language barriers to full and effective participation in mathematics, science, and social studies education—particularly for minority individuals. CAL's constituency is composed of private and public organizations with an interest in language practice and policy, including congressional offices, news organizations, executive agencies, and state and local officials.

Examples

1) ERIC (Education Resources Information Center) Clearinghouse on Languages and Linguistics. Operated by CAL under a contract from the U.S. Department of Education (§104), the clearinghouse provides a mechanism for the collection, organization, and broad dissemination of information about diverse aspects of language and linguistics to practitioners, policymakers, researchers, and the interested public.

2) National Clearinghouse on Literacy Education (NCLE), operated by CAL with assistance from the U.S. Department of Education's Office of Educational Research and Improvement (see §104), provides practical, timely information and technical assistance to practitioners, policymakers, and researchers concerned with diverse aspects of literacy education for limited-English-proficient adults and out-of-school youth. It issues *NCLE Notes*, published twice a year.

3) CAL is a reading promotion partner of the Center for the Book in the Library of Congress (§32).

Publications

Textbooks, training courses in printed and in video cassette form, fact sheets, newsletters, and bibliographers.

Sources of Support

Federal funds, publications, and foundation donations.

---

§31   Center for Book Arts

626 Broadway, 5th Floor
New York, NY 10012
212-460-9768
Fax: 212-475-0242
Richard Minsky, *President and Founder*
Brian Hannon, *Executive Director*
Established in 1974

What/For Whom

The Center for Book Arts is a nonprofit organization whose purpose is to promote and exhibit the art of the book, both traditional and contemporary. The center offers lectures, courses, workshops, and exhibitions relating to typography, hand bookbinding, papermaking, letterpress printing, and book production. Book and paper restoration, the construction of boxes and portfolios for conservation, and the history of the book are regularly taught in courses and weekend workshops. Avant-garde creativity in bookmaking is another focus of the center, which also offers printing and binding services and workshop and studio rental. The center also features an annual artist's members show.

Examples

1) The center's activities include courses in bookbinding, book restoration, hand papermaking, and letterpress printing and weekend workshops on box making, paper marbling, wood engraving, bookmaking, printing, and papermaking.

2) The Book Arts Gallery, located at the center, is one of the few galleries dedicated to the book arts.

Publications

koob stra, an occasional update from Center for Book Arts includes a national calendar of courses, lectures, and other events on the book arts and reviews of books on the same subject; catalogs of exhibitions; and a video catalog *Books in the Arts Is the USA.*

Sources of Support

Membership fees, contributions, and grants from foundations and the New York Council on the Arts.

---

§32 The Center for the Book in the Library of Congress

Washington, DC 20540-8200
202-707-5221
Fax: 202-707-9898
John Y. Cole, *Director*
Maurvene D. Williams, *Program Officer*
Established in 1977

What/For Whom

The Center for the Book in the Library of Congress was established by Act of Congress, Public Law 95-129, approved on October 13, 1977. It was created "to heighten public interest in the role of books and printing in the diffusion of knowledge." Within the Library of Congress (§64), the center is a focal point for celebrating the legacy of books and the printed word. Outside the Library, it works closely with other organizations to foster understanding of the vital role of books, reading, libraries, and literacy. It serves as a catalyst and a source of ideas—both nationally and internationally.

A partnership between the government and the private sector, the center depends on annual, tax-deductible contributions from corporations and individuals to support its projects, symposia, exhibits, and publications. Using private funds, it sponsors projects of interest to both the general public and scholars. Its major areas of activity are literacy and reading promotion, the role of books and reading in today's society, the international role of books, the recognition and celebration of America's literary heritage, and the history of books and print culture.

The catalytic function of the center has expanded dramatically since 1984 with the establishment of statewide, affiliated centers for the book in twenty-six states and a reading promotion partnership program that includes more than 120 national civic and educational organizations.

Examples

1) The National Reading Promotion Partners. In 1987, with "The Year of the Reader," the Center for the Book began a program of national reading promotion campaigns. Each year national organizations have been invited to participate. More than 120 educational and civic organizations have become the center's reading promotion partners for "Books Change Lives," the 1993-94 campaign. Partners develop projects that use the theme; or they publicize the project and their involvement with the Library of Congress in the effort; or they make a financial or in-kind contribution to the campaign. A complete list of these organizations, many of which appear in this directory, is available from the center.

2) "Read More about It," the CBS Television/Library of Congress book project, is a principal Center for the Book promotion effort. Since 1979, more than three hundred CBS television presentations have included a thirty-second message in which a performer mentions books suggested by the Center for the Book and sends viewers to their local libraries and bookstores to "Read More about It." Millions of viewers, for example, saw the messages during the 1992 Super Bowl game and the 1992 Winter Olympic Games.

3) "The Literary Heritage of the States," a three-year education program, features "Language of the Land: Journeys into Literary America," a traveling exhibit based on the Library's collection of literary maps. The project is supported by a grant from the Lila Wallace-Reader's Digest Fund.

4) "The Library-Head Start Partnership Project" is a collaboration with Head Start and the American Library Association (§12) that demonstrates how librarians who serve children and Head Start teachers can work in family literacy programs.

5) National Young Reader's Day. In cooperation with Pizza Hut, Inc., each November the Center for the Book sponsors National Young Reader's Day, a celebration of the joys of reading for young people.

6) The center is an affiliate member of the National Coalition for Literacy (§75).

48

7) The State Centers. The purpose of each state center is to stimulate interest in books, reading, and all parts of a state's book culture and literary heritage. Each state center develops and funds its own operation and projects. The centers use Library of Congress promotion themes and occasionally host its traveling exhibits. When its application is approved, a state center is granted affiliate status for a period of three years. Renewals are for three-year periods. The state centers are:

Alaska (1990), Cyrano's Bookshop, 413 D Street, Anchorage, AK 99501; telephone 907-274-2599

Arizona (1988), P.O. Box 34438, Phoenix, AZ 85067; telephone 602-265-2651; Fax 602-265-6250

California (1987), California State Library Foundation, 1225 Eighth Street, Suite 345, Sacramento, CA 95814; telephone 916-447-6331

Colorado (1988), Colorado State Library, 201 East Colfax, Suite 309, Denver, CO 80203; telephone 303-866-6876; Fax 303-866-6940

Connecticut (1987), Connecticut State Library, 231 Capitol Avenue, Hartford, CT 06106; telephone 203-560-8388; Fax 203-724-6299

Florida (1984), Broward County Library, 100 South Andrews Avenue, Ft. Lauderdale, FL 33301; telephone 305-357-7404; Fax 305-357-7399

Illinois (1985), Illinois State Library, 300 South Second Street, Springfield, IL 62701; telephone 217-782-0974

Indiana (1987), Indiana State Library, 140 North Senate Avenue, Indianapolis, IN 46204; telephone 317-232-3692

Iowa (1987), Public Library of Des Moines, 100 Locust Street, Des Moines, IA 50308; telephone 515-283-4152; Fax 515-283-4503

Kansas (1987), Topeka/Shawnee County Public Library, 1515 West Tenth, Topeka, KS 66604-1374; telephone 913-233-2040; Fax 913-233-2055

Kentucky (1992), Kentucky Department for Libraries and Archives, 300 Coffee Tree Road, Box 537, Frankfort, KY 40602-0537; telephone 502-875-7000; Fax 502-564-5773

Michigan (1986), Library of Michigan, P.O. Box 30007, Lansing, MI 48909; telephone 517-373-1580; Fax 517-373-5700

Minnesota (1990), Metronet, 226 Metro Square Building, Seventh and Robert Streets, St. Paul, MN 55101; telephone 612-224-4801; Fax 612-224-4827

Missouri (1993), Missouri State Library, P.O. Box 387, Jefferson City, MO 65102-387; telephone 314-751-3615

Montana (1990), Montana State Library, 1515 East Sixth Avenue-CAPNO 201800, Helena, MT 59620-1800; telephone 406-444-3115; Fax 406-444-4612

Nebraska (1990), c/o Lincoln City Libraries, 136 South Fourteenth Street, Lincoln, NE 68508; telephone 402-441-8516

North Carolina (1992), Division of State Library, NC Department of Cultural Resources, 109 East Jones Street, Raleigh, NC 27601-2807; telephone 919-733-2570; Fax 919-733-6910

North Dakota (1993), North Dakota State Library, 604 East Boulevard, Bismarck, ND 58505-0800; telephone 701-224-3681

Ohio (1987), The State Library of Ohio, 65 South Front Street, Columbus, OH 43266; telephone 614-644-7061

Oklahoma (1986), Oklahoma Department of Libraries, 200 Northeast Eighteenth Street, Oklahoma City, OK 73105; telephone 405-521-2502

Oregon (1986), Oregon State Library, State Library Building, Salem, OR 97310-0642; telephone 503-378-4367

Pennsylvania (1989), State Library of Pennsylvania, Room 217A, P.O. Box 1601, Forum Building, Harrisburg, PA 17105; telephone 717-783-5723; Fax 717-783-5728

Texas (1987), Dallas Public Library, 1515 Young Street, Dallas, TX 75201; telephone 214-670-1400

Virginia (1987), The Virginia State Library and Archives, Eleventh at Capitol, Richmond, VA 23219; telephone 804-371-6493

Washington (1989), Seattle Public Library, 1000 Fourth Avenue, Seattle, WA 98104; telephone 206-386-4184; Fax 206-386-4132

Wisconsin (1986), Wisconsin Academy of Sciences, Arts and Letters, 1922 University Avenue, Madison, WI 53705; telephone 608-263-1692; Fax 608-365-3039

Publications

Since 1978, the Center for the Book has sponsored the publication of over eighty books and pamphlets. Recent titles include *Developing Lifetime Readers: A Report on a National Reading Promotion Campaign; A Description of Descriptive Bibliography;* and *Jefferson's Legacy: A Brief History of the Library of Congress.* A complete list is available from the center.

Sources of Support

Tax-deductible contributions from individuals, corporations, and foundations, with administrative support from the Library of Congress.

---

§33 Center for the Study of Reading

University of Illinois
174 Children's Research Center
51 Gerty Drive
Champaign, IL 61820
217-333-2552
Richard Anderson, *Director*
Established in 1976

What/For Whom

The Center for the Study of Reading conducts basic research on the nature of reading and undertakes applied research on teaching techniques and instructional materials. The center develops new methods for teaching children and youth having trouble learning to read, and sponsors professional development programs for teachers. The center is staffed by researchers who represent a wide range of disciplines, including reading education, cognitive psychology, educational psychology, linguistics, computer science, special education, and elementary and secondary education. The researchers seek to further a better understanding of how people learn to read, how they comprehend what they read, and how they can be taught to read.

Besides conducting research projects, the center provides services for teachers and opportunities for doctoral students to work with senior researchers on many aspects of reading, and sponsors colloquia, conferences, and institutes.

Examples

1) The center administers the Reading Research and Education Center (RREC), established and supported by the U.S. Department of Education's Office of Educational Research and Improvement (see §104) to increase knowledge about education. The center's primary mission is to conduct basic and applied research activities in the teaching and learning of literacy, which will benefit practitioners and users. Focusing on higher order literacy skills, the center's research program addresses the acquisition of knowledge and skills, instruction in reading, text structure and testing of reading proficiency, and evaluation of instruction.

2) In conjunction with the annual national meeting of the International Reading Association (§61), the center sponsors a day-long conference focusing on current reading research.

3) The center cosponsored a children-and-books workshop with the AAP Reading Initiative (see §19), which resulted in a project to encourage the concept of showing more book reading on television programs aimed at young people and their parents.

Publications

Over five hundred technical reports have been prepared and are available through the ERIC (see §104) system. The center cosponsored the publication of *Becoming a Nation of Readers,* the report of the National Academy of Education's Commission on Reading. Other books and pamphlets are also available.

Source of Support

Grants and contracts from the U.S. Department of Education (§104) and other federal and state agencies and from private companies and foundations.

§34 Chautauqua Literary and Scientific Circle (CLSC)

Chautauqua Institution
Chautauqua, NY 14722
716-357-6232
Norman A. Pederson, *Acting Director*
Founded 1878

What/For Whom

The Chatauqua Literary and Scientific Circle, the oldest continuous planned reading program in America, was founded
on the primary objectives of never-ending education and
stimulating organized lifelong learning for men and women
of all ages and classes. CLSC offers home reading courses for
adults and young people who read alone or in groups. The
four-year course of books selected from the CLSC book list has
offerings in the fields of art, science, literature, religion, international affairs, Americana, sociology, and economics, with
extensive bibliography and program suggestions. CLSC grants
a diploma of recognition to those who report their reading.
The circle also sponsors summer class meetings and hosts an
annual recognition day.

Examples

1) CLSC has enrolled more than a million readers, and at one
time sponsored ten thousand reading circles throughout the
United States and in foreign countries.

2) The Chautauqua Institution is a reading promotion partner of the Center for the Book in the Library of Congress
(§32).

Publications

The Chatauquan, a periodic tabloid containing program information and schedules; *Round Table,* an annual; and *Book An-
nouncement and History Book List, 1878-1985.*

Sources of Support

Membership fees and sale of publications.

§35 Chicago Book Clinic

111 East Wacker Drive, Suite 200
Chicago, IL 60601-4298
312-946-1700
Fax: 312-616-0223
Cynthia Clark, *Executive Secretary*
Founded in 1936

What/For Whom

The Chicago Book Clinic promotes good craftsmanship in the
editing and production of books, offers courses in various
aspects of publishing, and organizes seminars, lectures, and

exhibitions related to publishing and publishing technology. The Book Clinic meets monthly and its interests extend to commercial, university, and small press publishing. Its annual exhibit of award-winning designs, one of the most prestigious in the nation, includes textbooks, scholarly books, and trade books for adults and children. The Chicago Book Clinic draws on a fifteen-state area and has over nine hundred members.

Examples

1) The clinic offers introductory courses in copyediting, book design, and other production areas.

2) The biennial exhibit "Pubtech" is an extensive and well-attended show on new technologies in publishing.

Publications

Bulletin Board, monthly for members; the catalog of its annual exhibit of award-winning designs; and an annual membership directory.

Sources of Support

Membership fees and contributions.

§36 Children's Book Council, Inc. (CBC)

568 Broadway, Suite 404
New York, NY 10012
212-966-1990
Fax: 212-966-2073
Paula Quint, President
Established in 1945

What/For Whom

The Children's Book Council, Inc., is a nonprofit association of publishers that encourages the reading and enjoyment of children's books. Its members publish children's and young adult trade books—books for independent reading, not textbooks. CBC's best known activity is its annual sponsorship of National Children's Book Week, celebrated each November on the week before Thanksgiving.

Besides preparing reading promotion materials, CBC promotes adults' understanding of children's literature and the use of trade books in child-related disciplines. Some of this programming is developed entirely by CBC; some of it through joint CBC committees with such professional organizations as the American Booksellers Association (§7), the American Library Association (§12), the International Reading Association (§61), the National Council on Social Studies, and the National Science Teachers Association. CBC makes available to the public the resources of its library, including examination copies of books recently published by its members and a professional collection of interest to children's book specialists.

Examples

1) The American Booksellers Association-CBC Joint Committee annually sponsors the exhibit and catalog *Children's Books Mean Business*, which brings booksellers' attention to children's books that publishers themselves select as having a special appeal.

2) The American Library Association-CBC Joint Committee has organized children's book exhibits and developed programs and preconferences at both ALA and CBC conferences. The committee was involved in two projects. The first was the production of "Building a Home Library," a series of four brochures that describe books available in both hardcover and paperback editions designed to encourage people to own family libraries. The second project was a national competition to recognize outstanding examples of cooperation between a youth library (school or public) and one or more business or community agencies in the library's community, resulting in increased interest in books and reading.

3) The International Reading Association-CBC Joint Committee compiles *Children's Choices*, an annual list of selected new titles read by children in school systems across the country.

4) The National Science Teacher's Association (NSTA)-CBC Joint Committee annually sponsors *Outstanding Science Trade Books For Children*.

5) The National Council on the Social Studies (NCSS)-CBC Joint Committee issues *Notable Children's Trade Books in the Field of Social Studies*, an annual list.

6) CBC is a reading promotion partner of the Center for the Book in the Library of Congress (§32).

Publications

CBC Features, a newsletter published twice a year, includes information on CBC activities, articles on children's books, and listings of free and inexpensive children's book promotion material available from CBC's publisher members. CBC also administers the preparation of annual booklists (including lists of children's books in the areas of social studies and science) and produces posters, bookmarks, and other display and promotional material created by well-known children's book illustrators and writers. Occasional reference and informational output includes pamphlets such as *Writing Children's Books* and *Illustrating Children's Books* and the updated bibliographic reference book *Children's Books: Awards and Prizes.*

Sources of Support

The sale of materials and publishers' membership dues.

54

§37 Children's Literacy Initiative (CLI)

320 Walnut Street, 2d floor
Philadelphia, PA 19106
215-574-2920
Fax: 215-574-1404
Linda Katz and Marcia Moon, *Cofounders*
Established 1988

What/For Whom
Children's Literacy Initiative is a nonprofit organization that serves caregivers and teachers of young children in developing a positive connection with children and quality literature. CLI promotes the literacy of low income and educationally at-risk children by working with families, caregivers, and teachers, as well as with administrators of day-care, Head Start, and other preschool programs. It conducts training workshops, develops training materials, publicizes issues and solutions for illiteracy with early intervention, and produces media events that promote children's literacy. The organization also serves as an advocacy group to share research on literacy issues dealing with children and promotes the adoption of regulations and standards for classroom book collections (and reading aloud) for day-care programs and early elementary grades.

Examples
1) The initiative produces "Mrs. Bush's Story Time," a national radio broadcast featuring the former First Lady reading aloud from children's books.

2) CLI sponsors Children's Expo, a two-day event in Philadelphia to encourage the community to learn about quality children's literature and the importance of reading aloud.

Sources of Support
Gifts from foundations, corporations, and the state government of Pennsylvania.

§38 Children's Literature Association (chLA)

22 Harvest Lane
Battle Creek, MI 49017
616-965-8180
Marianne Gessner, *Executive Secretary*
Established in 1972

What/For Whom
The Children's Literature Association is a nonprofit organization of teachers, scholars, librarians, editors, writers, illustrators, and parents interested in the serious study of children's

literature. The association is devoted to promoting scholarship and criticism in children's literature, enhancing the professional stature of the graduate and undergraduate teaching of children's literature, and encouraging high standards of criticism in children's literature. ChLA awards fellowships to assist members in research, presents annual awards, sponsors an annual conference, and conducts workshops on teaching literary criticism to children in kindergarten through eighth grade.

Examples

1) The Phoenix Award is given to an author of a book for children published twenty years earlier that did not win a major award at the time of its publication but which, from the perspective of time, is deemed worthy of special recognition for its literary quality.

2) Chla sponsors the Carol Gay Memorial Essay Contest to encourage students in grades seven through twelve to write quality essays about literature.

Publications

ChLA Quarterly, Touchstones: Reflections on the Best in Children's Literature, critical essays on classic works of children's literature, and other books and pamphlets.

Sources of Support

Membership fees, sale of publications, and private contributions.

§39 Children's Television Workshop (CTW)

1 Lincoln Plaza
New York, NY 10023
212-595-3456
Frances Kaufman, *Vice President/Public Affairs*
Established in 1968

What/For Whom

Children's Television Workshop is the world's largest independent producer of educational television programs. It uses mass media technologies and techniques to inform and educate children primarily outside regularly scheduled classes in school. The workshop's programs are widely available and are designed to appeal to special audiences such as minorities, the economically deprived, or those with handicapping conditions. Programs appear on Public Broadcasting System (PBS) channels.

Examples

1) Sesame Street, targeted for children between the ages of two and five, helps prepare preschool children for the transition from the home environment to the classroom by teach-

ing basic cognitive skills such as letters and numbers and social-emotional attributes such as pride and cooperation. Emphasis is placed on print literacy, prereading, writing, and vocabulary. Celebrity guests have included the first American female astronaut, Sally Ride, jazz performer Cab Calloway, violinist Itzhak Perlman, and actor and singer Harry Belafonte.

2) 3-2-1 Contact, focusing on children from eight to twelve years old, shows the diverse world of science and technology at work in new and interesting ways. Programs feature a company of young hosts who travel the world in search of scientific information.

3) Square One TV, designed for eight to twelve year olds, is part of a national effort to improve mathematics education. The program's goals are to promote interest in and enthusiasm for mathematics to encourage the use of problem-solving processes and to present a broad spectrum of mathematical topics.

4) Ghostwriter, developed for seven to ten year olds, is a reality-based mystery adventure series designed to make the printed word exciting and relevant to children. The goals of the program are to motivate children to enjoy and value reading and writing, to show children how to use effective reading and writing strategies, and to provide children with compelling opportunities to read and write.

5) CTW is a reading promotion partner of the Center for the Book in the Library of Congress (§32).

Publications

Children's Television Workshop publishes books for prereaders and early readers in cooperation with companies such as Random House and Western Publishing. The workshop publishes monthly children's activity magazines for its shows and produces records, videocassettes, toys and games, clothing, and computer software, which incorporates some of the same educational values as the television programs. For adults, CTW commissions special studies of audiences not covered by standard television audience statistics and publishes bibliographies of recent writings on workshop programming and research efforts.

Sources of Support

Product-licensing royalties, sale of periodicals and records, and overseas broadcast fees. Funds for creating new educational television programs are derived from government agencies, public broadcasting sources, foundations, and private corporations.

§40 Christian Booksellers Association (CBA)

P.O. Box 200
2620 Venetucci Boulevard
Colorado Springs, CO 80901
719-576-7880
Fax: 719-576-0795
William R. Anderson, *President*
Founded in 1950

What/For Whom

The Christian Booksellers Association is an international trade association of retail stores and suppliers of religious books. The CBA monitors and compiles statistics on the religious book trade and provides services to members through its publications program, regional meetings, and an annual national convention. The CBA presents awards, provides a placement service, and offers educational activities.

Examples

1) In 1987, CBA sponsored the publication of *Christian Book Publishing & Distribution in the United States and Canada—A Landmark Study of the Historical Context, Present Profile, Consumer Markets, and Key Trends in the 21st Century.*

2) The Christian Booksellers Association is a reading promotion partner of the Center for the Book in the Library of Congress (§32).

Publications

Bookstore Journal, a monthly; *Members Express*, a newsletter issued ten times a year; *Current Christian Books*, an annual; *Supplier's Directory*, an annual; and manuals useful to member bookstores.

Sources of Support

Membership fees.

§41 Contact Literacy Center

P.O. Box 81826
Lincoln, NE 68501-1826
402-464-0602
Fax: 402-464-5931
Toll-free literacy hotline: 1-800-228-8813
Toll-free GED hotline: 1-800-626-9433
Emily Herrick, *Director of Literacy Services*
Established in 1978

What/For Whom

The Contact Literacy Center is a division of Contact Center, Inc., an international nonprofit organization that offers referral and follow-up services in the areas of criminal justice and human services. The Literacy Center is the information and referral clearinghouse for the National Coalition for Literacy (§75), a national literacy network. Using a toll-free national hotline (staffed from 8 A.M. to 8 P.M. Monday through Friday, 8 A.M. to 12 noon on Saturday), the center responds to inquiries from throughout the country. The hotline provides information to three main groups. Prospective volunteer tutors receive a listing of literacy programs in their local area and information on how they can become involved. Corporate representatives receive information on how corporations can initiate or support literacy programs. Potential students who call are referred to literacy programs in their immediate area. A special cross-referral system, when authorized, enables the Contact Literacy Center to notify area literacy programs of the interest expressed by specific potential tutors, corporations, and students. Referrals can also be provided for adults and children with learning disabilities.

Example

The National Literacy Hotline was initiated in 1983. The number of inquiries increased from 31,000 in 1985 to more than 700,000 served in 1992.

Publications

The Written Word, a monthly newsletter, presents articles on literacy products, programs, and activities around the country. The center also publishes informational pamphlets on topics such as, literacy statistics, fund-raising for literacy programs, publicity for literacy programs, how to help your child succeed in reading, how to form a state or local literacy coalition, how to tutor without belonging to an organization, and libraries and literacy.

Sources of Support

Sale of its publications and individual, foundation, and corporate donations through the National Coalition for Literacy.

---

§42   Cooperative Children's Book Center (CCBC)

4290 Helen C. White Hall
University of Wisconsin-Madison
600 North Park Street
Madison, WI 53706
608-263-3720
Fax: 608-263-4933
Ginny Moore Kruse, *Director*
Established in 1963

What/For Whom

The Cooperative Children's Book Center is a research library for adults that collects children's and young adult literature. Its books do not circulate. CCBC's purposes are to provide a collection of current, retrospective, and historical children's books; to provide Wisconsin librarians, teachers, students, and others with informational and educational services based on the collection; and to support teaching, learning, and research needs related to children's and young adult literature.

The center receives review copies of almost all of the trade and alternative press books published in English in the United States for children and young adults. Each week, the center's staff examines the newly published books, reads many of them, and discusses the books formally or informally with other librarians and educators in Wisconsin and elsewhere in the nation. Through this process, CCBC makes selections for its annual *CCBC Choices*.

Examples

1) The 25,000-title CCBC library contains review copies of juvenile trade books, recommended children's trade books, historical children's books, books by Wisconsin authors and illustrators, contemporary and historical reference or bibliographic materials related to children's literature, and alternative press books for children.

2) A two-day children's literature conference is cosponsored every other year with CCBC funding units and the University of Wisconsin-Madison, Division of University Outreach.

Publications

CCBC Choices, an annual annotated bibliography of selected books for children and young adults; *Alternative Press Publishers for Children's Books: A Directory; Multicultural Literature for Children and Young Adults;* and bibliographies on selected children's literature topics.

Sources of Support

The Wisconsin Department of Public Instruction and the University of Wisconsin-Madison, with support for special projects from the Friends of the CCBC, Inc.

---

§43 COSMEP: The International Association of Independent Publishers

P.O. Box 420703
San Francisco, CA 94142-0703
415-922-9490
Fax: 415-922-5566
Richard Morris, *Executive Director*
Established in 1968

What/For Whom

COSMEP (Committee of Small Magazine Editors and Publishers) is the largest organization of independent publishers in the United States. It has more than fifteen hundred members.

The organization, whose aim is to increase promotion and distribution of member publications, markets titles from member publishers at the annual conferences of the American Booksellers Association (§7) and the American Library Association (§12) and holds its own annual national conference, which includes several days of intensive seminars on topics of current interest to publishers.

Example

COSMEP's all-day seminars have covered such topics as "Introduction to Publishing" and "The Legal Aspects of Publishing, Marketing, and Distributing."

Publications

COSMEP Newsletter, a monthly featuring extensive coverage of publishing and marketing opportunities in this country and abroad, provides a forum for the exchange of problems and solutions among its membership; also, *COSMEP Membership Directory*.

Sources of Support

Membership dues.

---

§44 Council for Basic Education (CBE)

725 15th Street, NW
Washington, DC 20005
202-347-4171
Fax: 202-347-5047
A. Graham Down, *President*
Established in 1956

What/For Whom

The Council for Basic Education, founded by a group of distinguished academic and civic leaders, is a national nonprofit organization whose objective is to strengthen teaching and learning in all of the basic disciplines: English (including reading and literature, writing and reasoning, speaking and listening), mathematics, science, history, geography, government, foreign languages, and the arts. The council's national programs promote teacher development, instigate restructuring of school curricula, and encourage the reform of current teaching and learning methods.

The council reaches its national network of leading educators, policymakers, school administrators, and citizens through articles and reports. It also conducts workshops, sponsors institutes, and awards fellowships.

Examples

1) Independent Study in the Humanities. The program offers fellowships for independent summer study to high school teachers of the humanities nationwide. The program was

established in 1982 by the council with a grant from the Division of Education Programs of the National Endowment for the Humanities (§80).

2) Teacher Institutes. These institutes keep teachers focused on program content in their fields and provide an opportunity for their intellectual renewal.

3) Writing to Learn Workshops. Intensive workshops train teachers to incorporate the use of writing into their instruction of all subjects, not merely English.

Publications

Basic Education, a monthly journal; *Perspective*, issued quarterly; and numerous books, reports, and occasional papers.

Sources of Support

Memberships and subscriptions, sale of publications, contributions from individuals and foundations, and government grants.

---

§45 Council of Literary Magazines and Presses (CLMP)

154 Christopher Street, Suite 3C
New York, NY 10014-2839
212-741-9110
Fax: 212-741-9112
Jim Sitter, *Executive Director*
Established 1967

What/For Whom

The Council of Literary Magazines and Presses, originally founded as the Coordinating Council of Literary Magazines, is a national nonprofit organization whose mission is to preserve, promote, and support independent literary magazines and presses. Members are primarily noncommercial literary magazines or presses that publish at least one issue or one book per year. The council's services and programs for members include technical assistance, research and development, advocacy, information services, and other initiatives. CLMP is the primary service organization and advocate in the field of literary magazines and presses.

Examples

1) The council's primary activities involve regranting projects. The Gregory Kolovakos Seed Grant Program bestows support to new literary magazines published in the United States.

2) CLMP and Poets & Writers, Inc. (§88) are cosponsors of the Literary Network (LitNet), a nationwide campaign to inform and mobilize the literary community on issues of freedom of expression and public cultural policy. The Literary Network operates from CLMP's offices.

3) The council administers the Literary Publishers Marketing Development Program, made possible by a grant from the Lila Wallace-Reader's Digest Fund, to strengthen the ability of literary magazines and presses to develop larger and more varied audiences through ambitious marketing initiatives.

Publications

CLMPAGES, a newsletter published irregularly, and the *Directory of Literary Magazines*, an annual.

Sources of Support

Membership dues and funding from foundations, corporations, government agencies, and individual donors.

§46   Council on Library Resources, Inc. (CLR)

1400 16th Street, NW, Suite 510
Washington, DC 20036-2217
202-483-7474
Fax: 202-483-6410
Internet: clr@cni.org (general)
W. David Penniman, *President*
Established in 1956

What/For Whom

The Council on Library Resources is a nonprofit operating foundation that helps libraries, particularly academic and research libraries, to make use of emerging technologies to improve operating performance and expand services. CLR interests include, along with advancing technologies, the economics and management of libraries and other information systems. In addition to grants for library management and the professional education and training of librarians, grants are given in the areas of preservation, access, and bibliographic services. The council's program concentrates on academic and research libraries because of their role in collegiate instruction, their centrality to research and scholarship, and what the council regards as "their fundamental importance to society." The council has also sponsored the development of international library programs.

Examples

1) The CLR Academic Library Management Intern Program is offered biennially to librarians who have an interest in the administration of large libraries and who wish to improve their management skills. An important component of the program is the willingness of directors and senior administrative staffs of large and well-managed libraries to become host institutions for the chosen interns.

2) The council sponsored the documentary film *Slow Fires: On the Preservation of the Human Record*, which focuses on the pres-

ervation of library and archive materials. The film was funded by the council, the Andrew W. Mellon Corporation, and the National Endowment for the Humanities (§80), with assistance from the Library of Congress (§64).

Publications

CLR Reports; also reports and brochures.

Sources of Support

Funding from private foundations and the National Endowment for the Humanities.

---

§47 Federation of State Humanities Councils

1600 Wilson Boulevard, Suite 902
Arlington, VA 22209
703-908-9700
Fax: 703-908-9706
Jamil S. Zainaldin, *President*
Founded in 1977

What/For Whom

The Federation of State Humanities Councils, a membership association of the state humanities councils, assists and complements the state councils in achieving their common mission: the integration of the humanities into American life. The federation has three goals: to build national support for the humanities and state humanities councils; to provide technical assistance, education, and information to state humanities councils; and to serve as a link between national organizations and state humanities councils to enrich national humanities programs. The federation monitors congressional legislation, serves as an advocate for the state councils and the humanities, sponsors training workshops, promotes and develops substantive humanities programs on a national level, and sponsors an annual conference that allows state council members and participants to exchange ideas on humanities programs.

Examples

1) The ACLS/Federation Task Force on Scholarship and the Public Humanities. This joint task force was created with the American Council of Learned Societies (§8) to strengthen public programs by learned societies and educational organizations.

2) The federation has cosponsored two literacy conferences with the Modern Language Association (§67).

3) The Betsy McCreight Award is presented to an individual for distinguished service to the public humanities and the state councils. The Helen and Martin Schwartz Award recognizes notable achievement at the state level.

4) The federation is a reading promotion partner of the Center for the Book in the Library of Congress (§32).

Publications   *Federation News*, published bimonthly, provides information on federation and state council activities, as well as humanities-related items of interest from around the country. Research reports, essays, and conference proceedings are also published.

Sources of Support   A grant from the National Endowment for the Humanities (§80), other federal grants, and membership dues.

---

§48   Freedom to Read Foundation

50 East Huron Street
Chicago, IL 60611
312-944-6780
Judith Krug, *Executive Director*
Established in 1969

What/For Whom   The Freedom to Read Foundation consists of librarians, lawyers, booksellers, educators, authors, publishers, and others concerned with preserving the First Amendment rights of freedom of thought and expression. The American Library Association (§12) organized the foundation to support and defend librarians whose positions are jeopardized because of their resistance to abridgments of the First Amendment and to assist in cases that may set legal precedents regarding the freedom of citizens to read. The foundation provides legal and financial assistance to authors, publishers, booksellers, librarians, teachers, students, and others who must go to court to defend this freedom. The foundation reports to the American Library Association on a regular basis on issues of censorship and freedom to read.

Example   A Freedom to Read "Honor Roll" has been created to recognize those who have played an active role in support of intellectual freedom through their defense of the First Amendment. The first awards were presented in 1988.

Publication   *Freedom to Read Foundation News*, published quarterly, includes articles and reprints on censorship trends, current court cases, legislative developments in Congress and at the state level, and news regarding battles against censorship by librarians and teachers.

Sources of Support   Membership dues and administrative support from the American Library Association.

§49 Friends of Libraries U.S.A. (FOLUSA)

1326 Spruce Street, No. 1105
Philadelphia, PA 19107
215-790-1674
Fax: 215-545-3821
Sandy Dolnick, *Executive Director*
Established in 1979

What/For Whom

Friends of Libraries U.S.A. is a national organization that works to develop and support local Friends of Library groups. Members include over three thousand Friends of Library groups, individuals, libraries, and corporations. An affiliate of the American Library Association (§12), FOLUSA holds its meetings in conjunction with ALA's conferences, administers a speaker's bureau, and presents annual awards to outstanding friends of libraries.

Examples

1) Twice a year, during the annual and midwinter ALA conferences, members of FOLUSA meet to share ideas and information.

2) One of FOLUSA's special projects is the Literary Landmarks program at which a landmark tied to a literary figure or work or its author is designated during a special ceremony or other public event. For example, during an ALA conference in San Francisco, the City Lights Bookstore in historic North Beach was dedicated with famed poet Lawrence Ferlinghetti, a co-founder of the bookstore, presenting remarks.

3) FOLUSA's "Books for Babies" project emphasizes to mothers of newborns the important role they play in the development of their children. Developed to help local friends groups start programs in their community, the project offers books and information about libraries and reading to mothers of newborns while they are in the hospital.

4) FOLUSA is a reading promotion partner of the Center for the Book in the Library of Congress (§32).

Publications

Friends of Libraries U.S.A. National Notebook, a quarterly, offers news of other friends activities; *Idea Bank*, a quarterly, includes special offers, program ideas, and materials available for friends; also, pamphlets and fact sheets.

Sources of Support

Membership dues, corporate support, sale of publications, and administrative support from the American Library Association.

§50 Graphic Arts Literacy Alliance (GALA)

c/o David Jacobson
President
The Gutenberg Society
P.O. Box 11712
Santa Ana, CA 92711
Founded in 1989

What/For Whom

The Graphic Arts Literacy Alliance is a nonprofit organization established to promote efforts to eliminate illiteracy, support existing and new literacy programs, and promote the cause of literacy throughout the graphic arts industry. The goal of GALA is to promote a more literate society through enhanced awareness of print media. GALA members include industry organizations, associations, and government agencies.

Examples

1) GALA's speakers bureau has member representatives of the industry who are available to speak at schools at all levels of education about their industry and the importance of print media and reading.

2) GALA conducts the "Print-Pals" children's writing contest, intended to interest young people in communications through writing and to develop an awareness of how the written word is converted into a printed and bound book.

3) GALA promotes Graphic Arts Literacy Month in November.

Publications

GALA News, published irregularly, and *Literacy and Print Media*, a ninety-page publication that covers topics ranging from family literacy to world literacy.

Source of Support

Membership dues and corporate support.

§51 Great Books Foundation (GBF)

35 East Wacker Drive, Suite 2300
Chicago, IL 60611-2298
312-332-5870
Toll-free: 1-800-222-5870
Fax: 312-407-0334
Alice Owen Letvin, *President*
Founded in 1947

What/For Whom

The Great Books Foundation is an independent, nonprofit organization that promotes a liberal education program for children and adults through reading and discussion of great works of literature. With close to 500,000 members, GBF supports discussion groups throughout the United States and has over sixteen series of readings. Each year, GBF trains more than 17,000 discussion leaders in two-day sessions that are held in all fifty states. Discussion groups normally meet every two weeks for adults and at various intervals for children. Titles discussed include ancient and modern classics of literature, philosophy, and other areas.

Examples

1) The Adult Third Series includes works from Shakespeare, the Bible, Thucydides, Chekhov, Homer, Chaucer, James, Aeschylus, Machiavelli, and Tolstoy.

2) The Junior Great Books Curriculum is a daily program of interpretive reading, writing, and discussion which is intended to help students reach their full potential as readers.

3) The Read-Aloud program for kindergarten and first grade children enables teachers and parents to work together in helping children learn to read and appreciate fine literature.

Publications

GBF publishes the series of paperback books used in Great Books discussion groups.

Sources of Support

Training fees, sales of books, and educational grants.

---

§52 Guild of Book Workers

521 Fifth Avenue, 17th Floor
New York, NY 10175
212-757-6454
Frank Mowery, *President*
Founded in 1906

What/For Whom

The Guild of Book Workers is a national nonprofit organization that represents the hand book crafts. Its members include hand binders, restorers, illuminators, calligraphers, private press printers, and makers of paper and decorated papers. The guild sponsors exhibitions and offers lectures, seminars, workshops, and discussion groups.

Example

The guild sponsors an annual two-day seminar on Standards of Excellence in Hand Bookbinding which offers workshops conducted by leading experts in the field. Tours of binderies, conservation facilities, rare book libraries, and papermaking establishments are regularly arranged in conjunction with the seminar. The proceedings are videotaped and made available to members who are unable to attend.

Publication	*The Guild of Book Workers Newsletter,* a bimonthly; a semiannual journal; a membership directory; and exhibition catalogs.
Sources of Support	Membership and workshop fees.

§53 Home and School Institute (HSI)

MegaSkills Education Center
Special Projects Office
1201 16th Street, NW
Washington, DC 20036
202-466-3633
Dorothy Rich, *President*
Established in 1964

What/For Whom

Home and School Institute is an independent, nonprofit educational organization that develops programs focused on the educational role of the family and on uniting all concerned with education—home, school media, business, social service agencies, unions, and organizations—in a circle of community support for schooling and student achievement. The work of the institute is based on research on how children achieve and families succeed. The institute's approach provides a guided tutoring role for families which complements but does not duplicate the work of the school. The HSI curricula are used by teachers and families directly in the classroom and at home and are keyed to prevention of drug and dropout problems. Family literacy and the needs of at-risk students are fundamental concerns of the institute.

Examples

1) MegaSkills Workshop Program, launched in 1989, teaches parents and guardians to help their children become ready to learn. Leaders are trained to conduct parent workshops sponsored by school systems, businesses, and community groups and held at schools, companies, churches and community centers.

2) To help meet the mandates of America 2000, HSI is engaged in two new initiatives: to increase literacy levels in families and to encourage families to help their children be prepared to learn.

3) The institute is a reading promotion partner of the Center for the Book in the Library of Congress (§32).

Publications

MegaSkills: The Power to Change Your Child's Life, provides information for families on how to teach important skills, including reading; *MegaSkills Parents Handbook,* issued in English/

Spanish and English-only, provides information for families on how to increase literacy levels; also handbooks, guides, and other tested resources.

Sources of Support   Grants from the federal government, foundations, and institutions and sale of publications.

---

§54   Home Mission Board of the Southern Baptist Convention

Literacy Missions Ministries
1350 Spring Street, NW
Atlanta, GA 30367-5601
404-898-7438
Fax: 404-898-7228
Kendale Moore, *Associate Director, Church and Community Ministries Department*
Established in 1959

What/For Whom   The Home Mission Board of the Southern Baptist Convention promotes and develops literacy training programs through Southern Baptist churches and associations around the country. Literacy is seen as a mission rather than a social service. The ministries train volunteer tutors to work in adult literacy programs, in programs for school-age children and youth, and in English as a second language.

Publications   *Handbook for Literacy Missions,* which outlines the ministries' rationale and procedures for teaching reading, writing, and conversational English, and other training resources.

Source of Support   The Southern Baptist Convention.

§55 Institute for the Study of Adult Literacy

The Pennsylvania State University College of Education
204 Calder Way, Suite 209
University Park, PA 16801-4756
814-863-3777
Fax: 814-863-6108
BitNet: ISAL@psuvm
Eunice N. Askov, *Director*
Established in 1985

What/For Whom

The Institute for the Study of Adult Literacy was established to promote a coherent and systematic means, as might be found in a university research community, to respond to the problems and issues related to literacy. Three major concerns of the institute are: study and research, improvement of practice, and advocacy and leadership.

Examples

1) The institute has developed and evaluated computer courseware for adult beginning readers and occupationally specific courseware: R.O.A.D. to Success to train commercial vehicle drivers and Job Trails to help unemployed or underemployed adults assess and improve basic skills for work.

2) The institute coordinates a statewide network of state-funded programs that train and place college students as literacy volunteers; runs several federally funded Student Literacy Corps and provides technical assistance to other federally funded corps.

3) In partnership with Project Learning U.S. (§90), WQED (Pittsburgh) and the Media and Learning Resource Division of WPSX-TV (Penn State University), ISAL works on Project Lifelong Learning, funded by the U.S. Department of Education (§104). The purpose of the project is to merge relevant research on characteristics of successful adult literacy programs in the context of the family, the community, and the workplace. The project includes public service announcements, documentaries, a teleconference, and a newsletter.

4) ISAL is a member of the National Coalition for Literacy (§75).

Publications

Mosaic: Research Notes on Literacy, published three times a year; reports; and conference proceedings.

Sources of Support

Grants from corporations and state agencies and sale of publications.

§56

International Board on Books for Young People (IBBY)

Nonnenweg 12, Postfach
CH-4003 Basel, Switzerland
4161 232917
Fax: 4161-272-2757
Leena Maissen, *Director of the Secretariat*
Founded in 1953

United States Board on Books for Young People, Inc. (USBBY)

c/o International Reading Association
800 Barksdale Road, P.O. Box 8139
Newark, Delaware 19714-8139
302-731-4218
Alida von Krogh Cutts, *Executive Secretary*
U.S. National Section of IBBY founded in 1958
USBBY formed in 1984

What/For Whom

The International Board on Books for Young People, composed of individuals, organizations, and public institutions that make up over fifty national sections, promotes international understanding through children's books. It encourages high literary and artistic standards for children's books and a wide distribution of books for children and young people, the establishment of national and international public and school libraries, and the use of literature in education. The biennial congresses of IBBY have focused on such topics as book illustration, books and the school, and children's literature and the developing countries. IBBY serves as an adviser to national and international groups and has consultative relations with UNICEF and Unesco.

The United States Board on Books for Young People is one of the national sections of IBBY. It encourages the provision of reading materials of merit to young people throughout the world and cooperates with IBBY and similar organizations. USBBY pays United States dues to IBBY. USBBY was formed in 1984 from two existing groups, the U.S. National Section of IBBY and Friends of IBBY, Inc. The American Library Association (§12) and the Children's Book Council, Inc. (§36) are charter patron members of USBBY; other members are dues-paying individuals, organizations, businesses, and foundations.

Examples

1) The Hans Christian Andersen Medals for children's authors and illustrators, created by IBBY and awarded biennially, is often called the "Little Nobel Prize."

2) IBBY initiated the observance of International Children's Book Day, which is customarily held on Hans Christian Andersen's birth date of April 2.

3) The "Books for Disabled Young People" collection has been exhibited by IBBY worldwide. This project was cosponsored with Unesco.

4) USBBY is a reading promotion partner of the Center for the Book in the Library of Congress (§32).

Publications

Bookbird, IBBY's publication of record, published quarterly; a semiannual newsletter from USBBY; the biennial IBBY Honour List; directories; proceedings; and catalogs.

Sources of Support

For both IBBY and USBBY, membership fees and contributions.

---

§57 International Book Bank, Inc. (IBB)

608-L Folcroft Street
Baltimore, MD 21224
410-633-2929
Toll-free: 800-US-GRANT (U.S. only)
Fax: 410-633-3082
Suzette Ungvarsky, *Acting Executive Director*
Founded 1987

What/For Whom

The International Book Bank, Inc. (IBB) is a nonprofit book-sending agency established to collect, sort, and ship appropriate donated books to needy recipients in developing and Eastern European countries. It seeks to identify reading needs and preferences in disadvantaged countries by encouraging recipients to participate as equal partners. Recipients select their materials from carefully annotated and computerized book lists. The book bank operates with a network of support from the American book industry through book donations from publishers, libraries, school boards, and individuals. Major partners and collaborators include the National Association of College Stores (§70), the U.S. Information Agency (§105), Unesco, the Peace Corps, World Book, Inc., the International Cultural Exchange, and the International Reading Association (§61).

Examples

1) IBB's Book List System, an inventory database, produces annotated book lists that encourage recipients overseas to choose the books they wish to receive.

2) IBB has received funding from the U.S. Information Agency (§105) to ship more than 300,000 books to Bulgaria, Czechoslovakia, Hungary, and Poland.

3) IBB conducted a Dialogue for Partners workshop in Baltimore in 1992 to generate interest in book donation programs and in current efforts to enhance the quality of donated book programs. A book based on the meeting, *Donated Book Programs: A Dialogue of Partners Handbook*, has been published.

4) IBB's "clearinghouse concept" was developed to encourage donations, to assist other book-sending agencies that lack warehouse space and computerized inventory systems, and to meet the growing number of requests for high quality educational materials from overseas.

5) IBB is a reading promotion partner of the Center for the Book in the Library of Congress (§32).

Publications

Building a Better World, a promotional video, focuses on IBB services and how the warehouse works; and, a presentation kit designed to explain IBB programs and services.

Sources of Support

Grants from the Canadian Organization for the Development of Education (CODE) and the U.S. Information Agency, in-kind book donations, and other contributions.

---

§58 International Book Committee (IBC)

1041 Wien
Mayerhofgasse 6
Austria
43-1-505-0359
Fax: 43-1-505-17-5450
Lucia Binder, *General Secretary*
Founded in 1972

What/For Whom

The International Book Committee is an advisory committee of nongovernmental organizations with consultative status to Unesco that are concerned with books and reading. Representatives of international organizations from throughout the book field—for example, the International Federation of Library Associations and Institutions (§59), International PEN (see §87), and the International Reading Association (§61)— are among IBC's eighteen member organizations. IBC was formed as an outgrowth of the 1972 International Book Year support committee and was instrumental in developing the declaration "Towards a Reading Society," which was adopted by the 1982 World Congress on Books in London. Reorganized in 1984, IBC's goal is to foster the creating of a reading environment in all types and at all levels of society, one of the targets set by the 1982 World Congress. IBC consults with Unesco on book matters and makes recommendations to governments and nongovernmental organizations. IBC awards an annual International Book Award for outstanding services rendered to the cause of books.

Sources of Support

Member organizations may sponsor delegates to meetings of the IBC.

---

§59 International Federation of Library Associations and Institutions (IFLA)

P.O. Box 95312
2509 CH The Hague,
Netherlands
31-70-140884
Fax: 31-70-834827
Paul Nauta, *Secretary General*
Founded in 1927

What/For Whom

The federation promotes international cooperation, research, and development in all fields of library activity including bibliography and information services. The multilevel membership includes national library associations and other library institutions, such as libraries, library schools, and bibliographic institutes. IFLA's current activities are in the areas of universal bibliographic control, universal availability of publications, preservation and conservation, and universal data flow and telecommunications. IFLA also devotes concentrated attention to Third World librarians in IFLA, sponsoring projects like an investigation of how to catalog African author's names and preparing curricula for training librarians in developing countries. IFLA has granted consultative status to a number of international organizations concerned with documentation and librarianship.

Examples

1) The Universal Bibliographic Control and International MARC program promotes the development and application of standards for the efficient international exchange of bibliographic information, particularly in machine-readable form. UBC's *International Cataloguing and Bibliographic Control* is published quarterly.

2) The Universal Availability of Publications program facilitates international access to hard-to-obtain publications. It

promotes national and international lending programs. The *UAP Newsletter* is published twice a year.

3) The Round Table on Research in Reading, established in 1986, is involved in two major projects: young people's reading in transition from childhood to adulthood and the image of the library in different countries.

4) The Children's Libraries Section sponsors Unesco's Books for All program to make the most effective use of available funds by supplying children's books to developing countries.

Publications *IFLA Journal,* a quarterly; *IFLA Annual, IFLA Directory,* and *IFLA Trends* (each published every two years); and other serial and monographic publications.

Sources of Support Funding from Unesco, the Council on Library Resources (§46), and national libraries and membership fees.

---

§60 International Publishers Association (IPA)

Avenue de Miremont 3
CH-1206 Geneva
Switzerland
41-22-463018
Fax: 41-22-475717
J. Alexis Koutchoumow, *Secretary-General*
Established in 1896

What/For Whom The International Publishers Association is a professional organization of national associations which represent publishers in each country. IPA's primary mission is to safeguard the fundamental freedoms to publish and to read. It defends the rights of authors and publishers to create and distribute the works of mind without hindrance while respecting the local and international rights attached to those works. The association is active in promoting campaigns to end illiteracy, encouraging wider availability of books throughout the world, promoting reading instruction and library development, and encouraging creativity and recognition of writers in every country.

Example IPA holds a congress every four years to discuss current issues affecting the international book trade, publishing, copyright, and related matters.

Publications *International Publishers Bulletin,* a quarterly, and brochures, reports, and congress proceedings. The association also sponsors *Rights: the International Journal of Copyright,* a quarterly published by the IPA Scientific, Technical, and Medical Copyright Committee.

Source of Support   Membership dues.

---

§61   International Reading Association (IRA)

800 Barksdale Road, P.O. Box 8139
Newark, DE 19714-8139
302-731-1600
Fax: 302-731-1057
Alan E. Farstrup, Executive Director
Established in 1956

What/For Whom

The International Reading Association is a nonprofit, professional organization that encourages the study of the reading process, research, and better teacher education; promotes the development of reading proficiency to the limit of each person's ability; and works to develop an awareness of the need and importance of reading as a lifetime habit. Its ninety thousand members include classroom teachers, reading specialists, administrators, educators of reading teachers, reading researchers, parents, librarians, psychologists, and others interested in improving reading instruction.

The association's more than eighty committees explore a variety of issues in literacy education: assessment, adult literacy, comprehension and learning, legislative action, learners with special needs, parents and reading, teachers as researchers, technology and reading, and whole language. IRA collaborates with other professional organizations to ensure joint action on political and social issues affecting reading and literacy education. Each year, the IRA holds a convention and presents more than twenty-six achievement awards in research, teaching, writing, and professional and community service.

Examples

1) The International Reading Association is a joint recipient, with the National Council of Teachers of English (§77) and Center for the Study of Reading (§33), of a grant from the U.S. Department of Education (§104) to develop national standards for reading, the language arts, and English.

2) The International Reading Association is a member of the National Coalition for Literacy (§75).

3) IRA regularly honors outstanding achievement in fields relating to reading and reading education. One award is the International Reading Association Literacy Award, presented by Unesco on International Literacy Day (September 8) each year for outstanding work in the promotion of literacy.

4) The Aging and Intergenerational Special Interest group promotes research on reading as it spans generations, the impact of early reading habits and interests of lifelong reading, the characteristics of adult reading, and intergenerational literacy programs.

5) The Family Literacy Commission was established to highlight the role school teachers and administrators can play in family literacy through their contacts with parents and to publicize the need for partnerships between schools and other organizations such as community and religious groups and business.

6) National Newspaper in Education Week, cosponsored annually by the IRA and the Newspaper Association of America Foundation (§85), focuses on using newspapers to teach young people to read.

7) IRA and the National Council of Teachers of English formed a joint task force to study literacy assessment and intellectual freedom and to suggest how these issues will affect and involve their membership.

8) IRA is a reading promotion partner of the Center for the Book in the Library of Congress (§32).

Publications

IRA's four professional journals are the *Reading Teacher*, for elementary school educators; *Journal of Reading*, for those concerned with the teaching of reading at secondary, college, and adult levels; *Reading Research Quarterly*, a technical journal for those interested in reading research; and *Lectura y Vida* ("Reading and Life"), published quarterly in Spanish by the Latin American office in Buenos Aires, Argentina. The bimonthly newspaper *Reading Today* contains news and features about the reading profession. Other publications include reports, bibliographies, critical collections, and other aids for the teacher, some in Spanish.

Sources of Support

Membership dues and fees for publications, advertising, and activities. Funds from private and governmental agencies support only special projects.

§62   KIDSNET

6856 Eastern Avenue, NW, Suite 208
Washington, DC 20012
202-291-1400
Fax: 202-882-7315
Karen W. Jaffe, *Executive Director*
Founded in 1984

What/For Whom

KIDSNET is a national nonprofit organization that provides information to the public sector about programs and initiatives produced and disseminated by the broadcast and cable industry that are targeted to children from preschool through high school. KIDSNET also works closely with representatives of the education, health, and social service communities. It develops print curricula on various topics that are targeted to this age group and used in conjunction with electronic media. This material is often disseminated directly to educational institutions or distributed by specific organizations or media outlets. KIDSNET conducts training workshops for educators, and health and social service professionals on subjects related to children and youth.

Information from the KIDSNET computerized clearinghouse is available in print as well as electronic formats to KIDSNET subscribers, which include schools and school systems, media centers and public broadcasting agencies, cable access stations, hospitals, and radio and TV and cable programmers and operators, producers, distributors, and researchers.

Examples

1) Subscribers can search KIDSNET by subject or curriculum area, target age, and special needs, such as bilingual materials, captioned in another language, or materials for the hearing impaired. Listings include literary references to books, plays, and short stories; availability of print materials, such as scripts and bibliographies; program formats, writers; and copyright requirements.

2) KIDSNET offers a Bulletin Board of projects and programs in development or in production for acquisition or instant monitoring of current and future competition in broadcast, cable, and home video markets.

3) KIDSNET is a reading promotion partner of the Center for the Book in the Library of Congress (§32).

Publications

A monthly bulletin, a calendar, a users guide, and a booklet, *TV with Books Completes the Picture.*

Sources of Support

Grants from foundations and corporations and subscription fees for access to online services.

§63   Laubach Literacy Action (LLA)

1320 Jamesville Avenue, Box 131
Syracuse, NY 13210
315-422-9121
Fax: 315-422-6369
Peter A. Waite, *Executive Director*
Established in 1955

What/For Whom

Laubach Literacy Action is the United States program of Laubach Literacy International, the oldest and largest non-profit, volunteer-based, adult literacy organization in the world. LLA combats adult and adolescent illiteracy nationwide by providing basic literacy instruction and English instruction for speakers of other languages, training tutors, publishing educational materials for students and tutors, providing referral services, and disseminating information on literacy.

Laubach Literacy Action specializes in working with literacy programs that provide instruction through trained volunteers. Its network of over fifty thousand volunteers provides tutoring to adult illiterates in forty-five states. Laubach uses its own textbooks and one-on-one method of literacy instruction. Nonreaders and low-reading-level adults not reached by other programs are special concerns of LLA. In addition to promoting adult literacy nationally, LLA has programs that work with community agencies, including public adult education agencies, social service organizations, churches, service clubs, libraries, and prisons. Volunteers are trained both to tutor and to administer programs.

Examples

1) Laubach Literacy Action is a member of the National Coalition of Literacy (§75).

2) LLA sponsors a biennial National Adult Literacy Congress, a forum for new reader representatives from fifty states.

3) LLA is a reading promotion partner of the Center for the Book in the Library of Congress (§32).

Publications

Literacy Advance, a quarterly newsletter; *Students Speaking Out,* for and by new readers; *Trainer Touchstone,* which contains information and specific techniques for preservice and in-service tutor training; *The Forum,* which addresses volunteer program management issues; and *State Update,* which contains news about funding opportunities, national events, legislative updates, and activities of state-level organizations. New Readers Press, Laubach Literacy International's United States publishing division, produces teaching and tutor-training materials aimed at new readers in community-based literacy programs.

| Sources of Support | Individual contributions, membership dues, publications income, and donations from corporations and foundations. |

---

§64   Library of Congress

Washington, DC 20540-0001
202-707-5000
Established in 1800

What/For Whom

The Library of Congress, the world's largest library, contains more than twenty million books and pamphlets and millions of manuscripts, maps, microforms, pieces of music, technical reports, photographs, and audio materials. It collects in most subjects and formats. Although benefiting from deposits to the Copyright Office of the United States, which is one of its departments, the Library of Congress does not contain a copy of every book printed in the United States. Nevertheless, in the spring of 1993, its collections numbered more than 100 million items. It is an international library, for it maintains six overseas offices, collects research materials in more than 450 languages, and exchanges publications with institutions around the world. It is estimated that two-thirds of the publications currently received by the Library of Congress are in languages other than English.

The Library of Congress offices with a specialized interest in the creation, preservation, and use of books or in stimulating public interest in books and reading include the Cataloging-in-Publication Division, the Children's Literature Center, the Copyright Office, the Preservation Directorate, the National Library Service for the Blind and Physically Handicapped, the Poetry and Literature Center, the Publishing Office, and the Center for the Book (§32).

Examples

1) The Cataloging-in-Publication Division, established in 1971, provides prepublication cataloging information to requesting publishers for those titles most likely to be acquired by U.S. libraries. For information, call 202-707-6372.

2) The Children's Literature Center, founded in 1963, provides reference, research, and bibliographic assistance to those interested in the media world of the child. The center also maintains professional relationships nationally and internationally with libraries, publishers, and other organizations concerned with the education and welfare of young people and it publishes the annual list *Books for Children*. For information, call 202-707-5535.

3) The Copyright Office administers the operation of the United States copyright law which protects the works of the nation's creative community, including authors, composers,

artists, and filmmakers. The office currently processes more than half a million new registrations each year. For information, call 202-479-0700.

4) The National Library Service for the Blind and Physically Handicapped, with a nationwide network of more than 160 cooperating libraries, supplies, at no cost, books and magazines in braille, disks, or cassettes together with playback equipment to a readership of over 700,000 including the visually and physically impaired of all ages. For information, call 202-707-5100.

5) The Poetry and Literature Center's mission is to foster and enhance the public's appreciation of good literature. Among its several programs, the center coordinates an annual literary season of public poetry, fiction and drama readings, performances, lectures, festivals, and symposia. The center also administers the programs of the poet laureate consultant in poetry. Since 1986, Robert Penn Warren, Richard Wilbur, Howard Nemerov, Mark Strand, Joseph Brodsky, Mona Van Duyn, and Rita Dove have served as poet laureates. For information, call 202-707-5394.

6) The Preservation Directorate is responsible for maintaining the information contained in the Library's diverse collections in usable condition over an extended period of time. It manages all strategic planning for preservation and focuses on conservation treatment of rare materials, on library binding activities, on preservation microfilming programs, and on research into new preservation technologies. Outreach activities include a preservation reference service, a publications program, and a staff and user education program. For information, call 202-707-5213.

Publications

Library of Congress Publications in Print, a biennial, is available without charge from the Library's Office Systems Services. It lists books, pamphlets, serials, folk and music recordings, literary recordings, and video recordings. Publications lists may also be available from individual divisions and offices.

Sources of Support

Federal government, supplemented by gift and trust funds.

§65 Literacy Volunteers of America, Inc. (LVA)

5795 Widewaters Parkway
Syracuse, NY 13214-1846
315-445-8000
Fax: 315-445-8006
Jinx Crouch, *President*
Founded in 1962

What/For Whom

The Literacy Volunteers of America, Inc., is a nonprofit organization that promotes and fosters increased literacy through serving those who are functionally illiterate or who have limited proficiency in English. Through a network of local affiliates, LVA offers training and support to individuals and other groups or organizations desiring to increase literacy through volunteer community-based programs. Literacy Volunteers has over 450 chapters in forty states. More than fifty thousand tutors and students are involved in its programs. One-on-one instruction is offered in both basic literacy and English as a second language. Literacy Volunteers of America recommends no single method or series of textbooks. The major emphasis in its publication program is on the development of training materials for program administrators, trainers, and tutors. LVA also provides technical assistance to beginning programs, disseminates literacy information, and provides referral services to potential tutors and students.

Examples

1) LVA shared a five-year Coors Foundation for Family Literacy grant with Laubach Literacy Action (§63) for cooperative work in serving literacy providers nationwide through the National Volunteer Literacy Campaign. The goal was to increase the number of trained volunteer tutors and to improve the support structures necessary for effective volunteer performance.

2) Wally Amos, LVA's national spokesperson, known for his "literacy awareness events," donated 5 percent of the royalties from his autobiography, *The Face That Launched a Thousand Chips*, and 10 percent of the profits from his second book, *Wally Amos's The Power in You* to support the work of LVA.

3) Video adaptations of the Basic Reading Tutor Training Workshop, financed by public and private funds, enable LVA to train more tutors in remote areas.

4) LVA is a member of the National Coalition for Literacy (§75).

5) LVA is a reading promotion partner of the Center for the Book in the Library of Congress (§32).

Publications   *The Reader*, a quarterly newsletter; several reading series; training manuals; handbooks; and reports.

Sources of Support   Sale of training and support materials; membership fees; fees for technical assistance to nonmember organizations; trust funds; government agency funding for projects; and contributions from foundations, corporations, and individuals.

---

§66   Magazine Publishers of America (MPA)

575 Lexington Avenue, Suite 540
New York, NY 10022
212-752-0555
Fax: 212-888-4217
P. Robert Farley, *Executive Vice President*
Established in 1919

What/For Whom   Magazine Publishers of America is the industry association for the consumer magazine business and is dedicated to defending the freedom to write and publish under the First Amendment. MPA serves as the primary source of information about the magazine publishing industry for both its membership, representing seven hundred magazines in the United States and over four hundred overseas, and for the community at large. Through its marketing, education, government affairs, and research programs, MPA works to support and promote the editorial and economic vitality of the magazine industry.

Example   MPA maintains an internship program in which college students are exposed to the inner workings of a magazine. The association regularly offers seminars on all aspects of magazine publishing and each year cosponsors the three-day American Magazine Conference with the American Society of Magazine Editors (ASME).

Publications   *Magazine*, a newsletter issued periodically; *Washington Report*, a monthly; and the *American Magazine*, copublished with the American Society of Magazine Editors, which commemorates the 250th anniversary of magazines in America.

Sources of Support   Membership dues.

§67 Modern Language Association of America (MLA)

10 Astor Place
New York, NY 10003-6981
212-475-9500
Fax: 212-477-9863
Phyllis Franklin, *Executive Director*
Established in 1883

What/For Whom

The largest organization of academic professionals in the United States, the MLA is devoted to the study and teaching of literature, languages, and linguistics. Its members are teachers, graduate students, journalists, librarians, administrators, poets, novelists, editors, translators, and other interested professionals, including independent scholars. The MLA provides leadership to the profession in curriculum, teaching, and faculty development through conferences and workshops in its English and foreign-language programs. It educates its members in the development and uses of new technology through publications and programs. It advocates the study of language and literature and the cause of the humanities to Congress, federal agencies, state and local governments, and the media.

MLA divisions encompass various time periods of English, American, and foreign-language literatures and varying approaches for studying them. The divisions include: Language and Society; Philosophical Approaches to Literature, including History of Ideas; and Children's Literature. Discussion groups are designed to accommodate the scholarly and professional interests of smaller constituencies within the organization, focusing on topics such as autobiography, biography, and lexicography.

Examples

1) MLA Committee on Academic Freedom. The committee takes action on issues of censorship and freedom of expression both within and outside of academe through public statements and the filing of amicus curiae briefs. For example, the committee opposes restrictions on books and instructional approaches and speaks out against threats to teachers' freedom of speech and employment.

2) MLA's annual convention each December provides members an opportunity to explore new avenues of research, discover connections between fields, and confer with scholars who share their interests.

3) As a member of the Joint National Committee for Languages with the American Council of Learned Societies (§8) and the National Humanities Alliance, MLA actively supports federal legislation funding literacy education, research librar-

85

ies, programs for manuscript and book preservation, grants for foreign language teaching, fellowships for scholars, and other endeavors benefiting research and teaching.

4) MLA is a reading promotion partner of the Center for the Book in the Library of Congress (§32).

Publications

MLA Newsletter, a quarterly, supplies information about the association and the profession. *PMLA*, a journal published six times a year, contains articles on scholarship and teaching. *Profession*, an annual anthology, publishes articles on professional and pedagogical topics. The *ADE Bulletin* (of the Association of Departments of English) and the *ADFL Bulletin* (of the Association of Departments of Foreign Languages) publish articles on professional, pedagogical, curricular, and departmental issues of concern to the profession as a whole. The MLA prepares and publishes many other publications.

Sources of Support

Membership dues, sale of publications, proceeds from conferences, Career Information Service fees, and sale of computer services.

---

§68   Multicultural Publishers Exchange (MPE)

P.O. Box 9869
Madison, WI 53715
608-244-5633
Fax: 608-244-3255
Charles Taylor, *Executive Director*
Founded in 1989

What/For Whom

Multicultural Publishers Exchange is a national organization of independent publishers representing black-owned and Hispanic presses as well as native American, Asian, and Pacific Islander presses. MPE was founded to improve networking with those who write, publish, and sell muticultural books and currently has more than 250 members. MPE promotes the dissemination of authentic information from and about different cultural communities and provides opportunities for professional exchange through trade representation, personal and professional referrals, conferences, and media networking. MPE also administers an awards program.

Example

MPE's Book Awards of Excellence Competition recognizes outstanding works of independent book publishers of color in three categories: fiction, nonfiction, and children.

Publications

MPE, a bimonthly newsletter, and an annual book catalog.

Sources of Support

Membership dues and subscription fees.

§69 National Association for the Preservation and Perpetuation of Storytelling (NAPPS)

P.O. Box 309
Jonesborough, TN 37659-0309
615-753-2171
Jimmy Neil Smith, *Executive Director*
Founded in 1975

What/For Whom

The National Association for the Preservation and Perpetuation of Storytelling is a nonprofit membership organization dedicated to encouraging a greater appreciation, understanding, and practice of storytelling. NAPPS is a resource for individuals and organizations wanting to know more about the art of storytelling, its meaning and importance, and its uses and applications in contemporary America as both an entertainment and an educational tool. The association sponsors a National Storytelling Festival every October, a National Congress on Storytelling in June, and a National Storytelling Institute.

Examples

1) NAPPS preserves the storytelling tradition through the National Storytelling Resource Center in Jonesborough, Tennessee, which houses archives of storytelling and video and audio tapes and serves as an information center for storytellers and those interested in the preservation of folkloric history and its perpetuation as a major art form.

2) The annual National Storytelling Festival is the oldest event of its kind in the United States. Established in 1973, this weekend of nonstop storytelling in Jonesborough celebrates storytellers, stories, and storytelling lore.

Publications

The Yarnspinner, issued eight times per year; *Storytelling Magazine*, a quarterly focusing on the history, uses, and applications of storytelling; *Storytelling Catalog*, a selection of storytelling resources; and the *National Directory of Storytelling*, an annual.

Source of Support

Membership dues.

§70 National Association of College Stores (NACS)

528 East Lorain Street
Oberlin, OH 44074-1294
216-775-7777
Fax: 216-775-4769
Garis F. Distelhorst, *Executive Director*
Established in 1923

What/For Whom

NACS is a trade association of retail stores that sell books, supplies, and other merchandise to students and faculties of educational institutions. Members also include publishers and suppliers to the college store market. The association was established to educate and aid college stores in achieving professional, profitable operations; to encourage open involvement and cooperation with college administration, faculty, students, and the community at large; and to promote greater awareness of the educational and financial contributions to their schools made by college stores. Though the association is nonprofit, it manages NACSCORP, a member-service, for-profit subsidiary that distributes books, computer software, calendars, and student-rate magazine subscription cards. NACS also conducts professional management seminars throughout the year for college store managers and sponsors an annual conference.

Examples

1) NACS promotes reading to the college market by encouraging member stores to do book promotions in conjunction with the American Library Association's Banned Books Week campaign (see §12). NACS also contributes to Reading Is Fundamental (§94), which focuses on children from the age of three through the high school years.

2) NACS has developed the "Bridge of Knowledge" book donation program, which provides donations from the publishing industry and hundreds of college bookstores to the International Book Bank, Inc. (§57).

3) NACS and the American Booksellers Association (§7) cosponsor a General Booksellers School, a professional-level school focusing on issues and topics of importance to both college and trade booksellers. Information on buying, industry trends, promotion techniques, and management is offered during three-day seminars.

Publications

College Store Journal, a trade magazine issued six times a year; *Campus Market Place*, a weekly that keeps members informed of developments and activities in the industry and the association or involving members; and *The Book Buyers' Manual*, issued every two years.

Sources of Support   Membership dues, seminar fees, sale of publications, and NACSCORP operations.

---

§71   National Book Foundation (NBF)

260 Fifth Avenue, Room 904
New York, NY 10001
212-685-0261
Fax: 212-213-6570
Neil Baldwin, *Executive Director*

What/For Whom   The National Book Foundation is a nonprofit organization that encourages reading and participation in the literary arts through making writers and books newsworthy and exciting to the general public. First established in 1955 and known as first the National (1955-80) and then the American Book Awards (1981-86), the organization became the National Book Foundation in 1989. The foundation raises funds to support literary programs in communities around the country in which authors both talk about their work and give readings. It administers the National Book Awards and sponsors several initiatives aimed at literary excellence and encouraging literacy among readers of all ages.

Examples   1) The National Book Awards were established in 1950 to honor literary works of exceptional merit. The NBF presents the awards annually for works of fiction, nonfiction, and poetry.

2) The NBF administers the "Writing Life" project, which brings National Book Award winners and finalists to communities across the country, where they discuss, in a variety of settings, the aims and inspirations behind their work. The project is supported by the Lila Wallace-Reader's Digest Fund.

3) The NBF sponsors National Book Week; in cooperation with the Center for the Book in the Library of Congress (§32) and other organizations. This annual celebration of writers and books takes place the third week of January.

4) The NBF and the American Booksellers Association (§7) collaborated to present a backlist promotion campaign designed to bring over two hundred award-winning books to the attention of a broader reading public.

5) The NBF is a reading promotion partner of the Center for the Book in the Library of Congress (§32).

Publications   *The National Book Awards: Forty-one Years of Literary Excellence; Winners and Finalists; 1950-1991; National Book Award Winners, Books in Print, 1950-1991*; and other publications.

Sources of Support   Grants from foundations and contributions from corporations and individuals.

§72 National Center for Family Literacy (NCFL)

Waterfront Plaza, Suite 200
325 West Main Street
Louisville, KY 40202-4251
502-584-1133
Fax: 502-584-0172
Sharon Darling, *President*
Established in 1989

What/For Whom

The National Center for Family Literacy is a private, nonprofit corporation created to expand efforts to solve the nation's literacy problems, with special emphasis on breaking the cycle of illiteracy through family intervention. It was established with a grant from William R. Kenan, Jr., Charitable Trust. The center provides a cadre of leaders, knowledgeable and skilled in education and family intervention techniques, who provide training and technical assistance to enable the establishment of quality family literacy programs throughout the nation. The center also encourages a national understanding and response to the cyclical problem of illiteracy through assistance and information provided to federal, state, and local policymakers and program planners. It supports the expansion of existing and developing family literacy efforts nationwide through training, material development, newsletters, conferences and seminars, and a clearinghouse function. NCFL also funds model programs and conducts research to ensure that practice informs research and that research improves the quality of family literacy efforts.

Examples

1) The NCFL is a partner with the Bureau of Indian Affairs in providing training and technical assistance in family literacy programs operating on Indian reservations in Washington, Minnesota, South Dakota, and New Mexico.

2) With an initial grant from Toyota Motor Corporation, NCFL established the Toyota Families for Learning program with family literacy programs in ten American cities and expanding to other cities. Structured like other NCFL programs, the Toyota endeavor provides for undereducated parents to work toward increasing their literacy and life skills while their children attend preschool under the same roof. The goal is for parents and children to develop as partners in learning and success.

3) The NCFL is a member of the National Coalition for Literacy (§75).

4) The NCFL is a reading promotion partner of the Center for the Book in the Library of Congress (§32).

Publications

The NCFL Letter, a quarterly; research reports; studies; and videotapes of center programs.

Sources of Support   Grants from foundations and individual and corporate contributions.

---

§73   National Center on Adult Literacy (NCAL)

Literacy Research Center
University of Pennsylvania
3910 Chestnut Street
Philadelphia, PA 19104-3111
215-898-2100
Fax: 215-898-9804
Internet e-mail: mailbox@literacy.upenn.edu
Daniel A. Wagner, *Director*
Established in 1990

What/For Whom   The National Center on Adult Literacy was established, through a grant from the U.S. Department of Education's Office of Educational Research and Improvement (§104), to enhance knowledge about adult literacy, improve the quality of research and development in the field, and ensure a strong, two-way relationship between research and practice. Central to NCAL's mission and work is the establishment of connections across the multiple communities and disciplines involved with adult literacy in the United States and abroad.

The center disseminates information through client-centered, self-sustaining networks within the educational, research, and business communities. The center sponsors roundtables, conferences, and workshops and participates in major conferences at the national, state, and local levels. NCAL's research and development affiliates include: the Center for Applied Linguistics (§30), City University of New York, the Educational Testing Service, Indiana University, Johns Hopkins University, the National Center for Family Literacy (§72), Northwest Regional Educational Laboratory, Pelavin Associates, University of California at Santa Barbara, and the University of Delaware.

Examples   1) The NCAL sponsors roundtables on adult learning and work, literacy and work, second language literacy, and literacy policy forums cosponsored with the Center for the Book in the Library of Congress (§32).

2) The NCAL administers a Dissertation Awards Program (DAP) which is designed to support and disseminate the findings of the best doctoral dissertations in the area of adult literacy, thereby strengthening research and development in that field.

Publications   *NCAL Connections*, a newsletter that provides summaries of all NCAL projects and a technical report series.

Sources of Support   Federal cofunding by the U.S. Departments of Education, Labor, and Health and Human Services.

---

§74 National Coalition Against Censorship (NCAC)

275 Seventh Avenue
New York, NY 10001
212-807-6222
Fax: 212-807-6245
Leanne Katz, *Executive Director*
Established in 1974

What/For Whom   The National Coalition Against Censorship is an alliance of national nonprofit organizations, including religious, educational, professional, artistic, labor, and civil rights groups, committed to defending freedom of thought, inquiry, and expression. The NCAC educates its own members about the dangers of censorship and how to oppose them and uses the mass media to inform the general public about censorship issues. Other coalition activities include conferences, program assistance, advocacy, and the monitoring of legislation with First Amendment implications at both national and state levels. The NCAC compiles and disseminates educational material, including information packets on many First Amendment-related issues, among them creationism, women and pornography, guidelines for selecting educational materials, government secrecy, and censorship and black literature.

Example   The coalition's Clearinghouse on School Book-Banning Litigation collects and makes available to librarians, journalists, lawyers, educators, school boards, parents, and the public at large up-to-date information on the status of school censorship cases and appropriate legal documents.

Publications   *Censorship News*, a quarterly newsletter; *Books on Trial: A Survey of Recent Cases*, a source of information on litigation arising from censorship in private schools in the United States, with a listing of books, magazines, and films involved; and *NCAC Books of the Month*, which lists challenged books the NCAC has been defending as part of an expanded program to counter censorship in schools and libraries; and periodic reports and background papers.

Sources of Support   Individual contributions, sale of publications, conference fees, and grants.

§75   National Coalition for Literacy

50 East Huron Street
Chicago, IL 60611
312-944-6780
Toll-free literacy hotline: 800-228-8813 (Contact Literacy Center)
Mattye Nelson, *Staff Liaison, American Library Association*
Established in 1981

What/For Whom

The National Coalition for Literacy was founded by the American Library Association (§12) to help unify efforts to increase national awareness of the problem of illiteracy. Some of the coalition's objectives include: providing a mechanism for regular communications among member organizations; stimulating, reviewing, and guiding public awareness campaigns targeted to particular populations or purposes; establishing policies for the operation of continuous literacy information and referral services; and providing a forum for the discussion of new national literacy initiatives.

The coalition's network includes member organizations that play a role nationally and locally in the delivery of literacy information and services: ACTION (§1), Adult Literacy and Technology Project, American Association for Adult and Continuing Education (§4), American Bar Association, American Council on Education, American Library Association (§12), Association for Community-Based Education (§18), Center for the Book in the Library of Congress (§32), Contact Center, Inc. (see §41), Correctional Education Association, Institute for the Study of Adult Literacy (§55), International Reading Association (§61), Laubach Literacy Action (§63), Literacy Volunteers of America (§65), National Alliance of Business, National Association of University Women, National Center for Family Literacy (§72), National Center on Adult Literacy (§73), National Commission on Libraries and Information Science (§76), National Council of State Directors of Adult Education, National Governors Association, National Rural Electric Cooperative Association, Newspaper Association of America Foundation (§85), Project Learning U.S. (§90), Student Coalition for Action in Literacy Education (SCALE), U.S. Department of Education (§104), U.S. Department of Labor, U.S. Postal Service, and United Way of America. The membership administers the coalition on a rotation basis.

Examples

1) Toll-free literacy hotline. The coalition considers the hotline essential for its continuing efforts to mobilize resources and recruit volunteers and students. Staffed by the Contact Literacy Center (§41), the hotline provides information on the extent of adult literacy and refers callers to local, regional, and state literacy programs for recruitment.

93

2) The coalition presents its Advancement of Literacy award to individuals who have made sustained outstanding contributions to the national adult literacy movement.

Sources of Support   Contributions from membership organizations.

---

§76   National Commission on Libraries and Information Science (NCLIS)

1110 Vermont Avenue, NW, Suite 820
Washington, DC 20005
202-609-9200
Fax: 202-606-9203
Peter R. Young, *Executive Director*
Established in 1970

What/For Whom   The National Commission on Libraries and Information Science is a permanent, independent agency of the United States government, established by Public Law 91-345, and charged with advising the president and Congress on national library and information policies and plans. The commission conducts studies, surveys, and analyses of the nation's library and information needs; appraises the adequacies and deficiencies of current resources and services; promotes research and development activities; conducts hearings and issues publications as appropriate; and develops overall plans for meeting national library and information needs and for coordination of activities at the federal, state, and local levels.

Examples   1) NCLIS planned and conducted the second White House Conference on Library and Information Services (WHCLIS) in 1991 and is the lead agency to develop plans and policies to carry out the ninety-five conference recommendations for library and information services in the twenty-first century.

2) NCLIS sponsors open forums on issues and topics of concern to the library and information services community. Some of these forums have addressed the role of libraries in the National Research and Education Networks (NREN), the role of national associations in the implementation of the WHCLIS 1991 recommendations, future federal roles for libraries, and relationships between public and private sector information concerns.

3) In a cooperative project, NCLIS and the National Center for Education Statistics (see §104) collected and compiled, for the first time, statistical data on all U.S. public libraries.

4) The commission cosponsored, with the American Association of School Librarians (see §12), a symposium "Information Literacy and Education for the 21st Century" which urged adoption of principles and practices to restructure the learning process into resource-based, lifelong education.

5) NCLIS formed a task force to address jointly the issues raised at a 1989 NCLIS hearing on the status of library and information services to native Americans. Subsequent regional hearings generated information and statistics for a long-range plan to improve library and information services for this population.

6) NCLIS is a partner in the National Coalition for Literacy (§75).

7) NCLIS is a cosponsor with the American Library Association (§12) of the National Library Card Sign-up campaign.

8) NCLIS is a reading promotion partner of the Center for the Book in the Library of Congress (§32).

Publications Reports, articles, and special publications.

Sources of Support Federal government.

---

§77 National Council of Teachers of English (NCTE)

1111 Kenyon Road
Urbana, IL 61801
217-328-3870
Fax: 217-328-9645
Miles Myers, *Executive Director*
Established in 1911

What/For Whom The National Council of Teachers of English is a nonprofit professional service organization committed to improving the teaching of literature and the English language. The NCTE emphasizes the need to teach English as both a system of language skills and a humane discipline. Its more than 120,000 members are English teachers, teacher educators, and researchers. The council provides information on the English and language arts teaching profession and offers direction and guidance to its members through a variety of publications, journals, conventions, conferences, and workshops.

Examples 1) The council sponsors achievement awards for excellence in writing, student literary magazines, and English language arts programs.

2) Faculty and graduate students in writing programs at two-and four-year colleges attend NCTE's annual convention of the Conference on College Composition and Communication.

3) The NCTE is a reading promotion partner of the Center for the Book in the Library of Congress (§32).

Publications

College English, a monthly aimed at the college scholar and teacher; *English Journal,* a monthly with the latest developments in teaching reading at the middle, junior high, and senior high school levels and short articles on concerns such as censorship, trends, and testing; *Language Arts,* a monthly for elementary school reading and language teachers and teacher trainers; *SLATE Newsletters,* issued six times a year, summarizing national news affecting English language arts educators; *Quarterly Review of Double Speak,* including articles, book reviews, and other materials dealing with double speak; and pamphlets, books, newsletters, cassettes, and other professional journals.

Sources of Support

Membership dues, sale of publications, conference fees, and individual contributions.

---

§78 National Council on the Aging, Inc. (NCOA)

409 Third Street, SW
Washington, DC 20024
202-479-1200
Fax: 202-479-0735
Sylvia Liroff, *Manager—Older Adult Education*
Established in 1950

What/For Whom

The National Council on the Aging is a private, nonprofit organization that serves as a major resource for information, training, technical assistance, advocacy, publication, and research on every aspect of aging. Individual members range from senior center professionals, health care practitioners, and other service providers to gerontologists, agency board members, and personnel directors. Organizational members include adult day- care centers; senior housing facilities; senior centers; older work employment services; and local, state, and national organizations and companies serving the aging.

Examples

1) NCOA's Discovery through the Humanities Program is a reading-centered, community discussion program for older adults that focuses on the humanities. At senior centers, public libraries, museums, housing complexes, residential care centers, churches, and synagogues across the country, older

people come together to actively explore the creative visions of distinguished writers and poets, thinkers, artists, and historians. The program, begun in 1976 and known formerly as the Senior Center Humanities Program (SCHP), is supported by a grant from the General Programs Division of the National Endowment for the Humanities (§80). Additional funding comes from participating senior centers, libraries, and sponsoring agencies and from corporations and foundations.

2) The Literacy Education for the Elderly Project (LEEP), produced a number of valuable resources to train and assist older volunteers serving as reading instructors to older individuals seeking literacy education. This project was begun and actively supported through the 1980s by a grant from the Fund for the Improvement of Postsecondary Education (FIPSE), an agency of the U.S. Department of Education (§104). Three publications and a VHS-format video are currently available for purchase.

3) NCOA is a reading promotion partner of the Center for the Book in the Library of Congress (§32).

Publications

Perspective on Aging, issued bimonthly, explores significant developments in the field of aging through opinion articles, profiles, book reviews, and editorials. *Abstracts in Social Gerontology: Current Literature on Aging,* a quarterly, provides detailed abstracts for recent major journal articles, books, reports, and other materials on many facets of aging. *NCOA Networks,* a bimonthly newspaper, highlights important developments and research in aging, current policy issues, and NCOA activities. NCOA has also developed a series of publications to help organize literacy programs especially for older adults.

Sources of Support

Grants from the federal government and foundations, membership dues, contributions from participating organizations, conferences, and sale of program guidebooks, software computer programs, and publications.

---

§79 National Endowment for the Arts (NEA)

Nancy Hanks Center
1100 Pennsylvania Avenue, NW
Washington, DC 20506
202-682-5400
Established in 1965

What/For Whom

The National Endowment for the Arts is an independent federal agency established to encourage and assist the nation's cultural resources. The Arts Endowment carries out its mission through grant programs and a wide range of leadership and advocacy activities. It also serves as a national forum to assist in the exchange of ideas and as a catalyst to promote the best developments in the arts and education. The NEA's mission is accomplished through fellowships awarded to individuals of exceptional artistic talent and grants awarded to nonprofit cultural organizations representing the highest quality in such fields as design arts, education, dance, folk arts, literature, media arts, museums, music, opera, theater, and the visual arts.

The Literature Program's purpose is to assist individual creative writers of excellence or promise, encourage wider audiences for contemporary literature, and help support nonprofit organizations that foster literature as a professional pursuit. Contact Gigi Bradford, Director, Literature Program, 202-682-5451.

Examples

1) The Literature Program awards fellowships for creative writers in fiction, poetry, and other creative nonfiction.

2) Literary publishing. Grants from Assistance to Literary Magazines help noncommercial literary journals that publish contemporary creative writing. Small Press Assistance grants support noncommercial literary small presses and university and college presses that publish contemporary creative writing.

3) Audience development. The Residences for Writers and Reading series supports residencies and reading series for published writers of poetry, fiction, and creative nonfiction; performance poets; and translators. The NEA is especially interested in projects that support literary programs in communities and populations traditionally underserved.

Publications

Arts Review, a quarterly review of developments in the arts and progress on endowment-supported projects, and grant application information, available from specific discipline programs.

Source of Support

Federal government.

§80 National Endowment for the Humanities (NEH)

Nancy Hanks Center
1100 Pennsylvania Avenue, NW
Washington, DC 20506
202-606-8271
Established in 1965

What/For Whom

The National Endowment for the Humanities is an independent federal agency established to promote the humanities through grants to humanities projects and scholars in defined areas of humanistic study. These areas include, but are not limited to, "languages, both modern and classical; linguistics; literature; history; jurisprudence; philosophy; archaeology; comparative religion; ethics; the history, criticism, and theory of the arts; those aspects of the social sciences which have humanistic content and employ humanistic methods; and the study and application of the humanities to the human environment with particular attention to the relevance of the humanities to the current conditions of national life." NEH grants are made through six divisions: Education Programs, Fellowships and Seminars, Preservation and Access, Public Programs, Research Programs, and State Programs; and through the Office of Challenge Grants.

Examples

1) The Division of Preservation and Access supports projects that will improve and increase the availability of resources important for research, education, and public programming in the humanities. Those may include books, journals, newspapers, archives, maps, photographs, film, sound recordings, and objects of material culture held by libraries, archives, museums, historical organizations, and other repositories. Contact George F. Farr, Jr., Director, at 202-606-8570.

2) The Division of Fellowships and Seminars supports scholars, teachers, and others undertaking independent research. Contact Marjorie A. Berlincourt, Director, at 202-606-8458.

3) The Division of Public Programs includes:

a) Humanities Projects in Libraries and Archives, which supports programs to enhance public appreciation and understanding of the humanities through the use of books and other resources in the collections of American libraries and archives. Projects supported include book discussion programs, lectures, symposia, and interpretive exhibitions of books, manuscripts, and other library resources. Contact Thomas C. Phelps, Program Officer, at 202-606-8267.

b) Humanities Projects in Media, which involves the planning, writing, or production of television and radio pro-

grams in the humanities intended for general audiences.
Contact James Dougherty, Program Officer, at 202-606-
8278.

4) The Division of Research Programs includes the Reference
Materials program, which funds the preparation of reference
works that will improve access to information and resources.
Contact J. Rufus Fears, Director, at 202-606-8200. For informa-
tion about NEH subventions for scholarly publications, contact
Margo Backus, at 202-606-8207.

5) The Division of State Programs supports humanities programs in individual states. Grants are awarded through a
network of humanities councils. Contact Carole Watson, Director, at 202-606-8254.

Publications

Humanities is a bimonthly review of current work and thought
in the humanities, which also describes recent grants and
progress on projects supported by endowment funding. In
addition, NEH publishes grant application information and a
variety of special publications.

Source of Support

Federal government.

---

§81 National Information Standards Organization (NISO)

P.O. Box 1056
Bethesda, MD 20827
301-975-2814
fax: 301-869-8071
Patricia Harris, *Executive Director*
Established in 1939

What/For Whom

The National Information Standards Organization, originally
created as Committee Z39 of the American National Standards Institute (ANSI), is a nonprofit association which develops technical standards used in a wide range of information
services and products. The standards address the communication needs of libraries, information services, publishing, and
the book trade in such areas as: information transfer, forms
and records, identification systems, publication formats, trans-
literation, preservation of materials, and library equipment
and supplies. NISO's more than sixty members include libraries; professional, technical, and educational associations;
abstracting and indexing services; publishers; government
agencies; and commercial and industrial organizations. NISO
participates in the International Organization for Standardization (ISO). Over twenty projects are in progress, some which

involve the development of entirely new standards and others the revision of older ones. The NISO Archives are located in the University of Maryland Library where they are accessible to qualified researchers and students.

Examples

1) NISO promotes and encourages the use of the infinity symbol inside a circle ∞ as the symbol identifying a publication printed on paper that will last several hundred years that meets the criteria for permanence set forth in the NISO-developed standard Z39.48.

2) The international standard book number, ISBN, and international standard serial number, ISSN, which facilitate the handling of books and periodicals at all levels of distribution, were defined by Z39 standards.

Publications

Information Standards Quarterly (ISQ), the official NISO newsletter, provides ongoing information about current standards developments. *NISO Standards,* an eight-page brochure listing all of NISO's standards, is available without cost.

Sources of Support

Membership fees and grants from the federal government and from foundations.

---

§82 National Institute for Literacy

800 Connecticut Avenue, NW, Suite 200
Washington, DC 20202-7560
202-632-1500
Fax: 202-632-1512
Lillian Dorka, *Acting Interim Director*
Established in 1992

What/For Whom

The National Institute for Literacy is an independent agency established by the National Literacy Act of 1991 (P.L. 102-73) to support the National Education Goal for Adult Literacy and Lifelong Learning: that by the year 2000, every adult will be literate and skilled enough to compete in the global economy and exercise the rights of citizenship. The institute is governed by an interagency group that consists of the secretaries of education, health and human services, and labor.

To improve and expand the system for delivery of literacy services, the institute assists federal agencies in setting specific objectives and planning strategies to meet the goals of the act and in measuring the progress of agencies in meeting such goals; conducts basic and applied research and demonstrations on literacy in adult basic education, literacy in the workplace, and family literacy; and provides assistance to federal, state, and local agencies and business and labor organizations in the development, implementation, and evaluation of literacy policy by providing technical and policy assistance for the improvement of policy and programs and establishing a national literacy data base.

The National Institute for Literacy also provides program assistance for literacy programs throughout the United States to improve the effectiveness and increase the numbers of such programs; collects and disseminates information to federal, state, and local entities with respect to literacy methods that show great promise; reviews and makes recommendations regarding ways to achieve uniformity in reporting requirements; develops performance measures; develops standards for effectiveness of literacy-related federal programs; awards fellowships to outstanding individuals pursuing careers in adult education and literacy; and provides a toll-free, long-distance telephone line for literacy providers and volunteers.

Examples

The institute issues grants which support basic and applied research and demonstration projects that support innovation in literacy and basic skills programs.

Publications

Literacy News, published irregularly.

Sources of Support

Federal government.

---

§83 National Parent Teacher Association (National PTA)

700 North Rush Street
Chicago, IL 60611-2571
312-787-0977
Fax: 312-787-8342
Tari Marshall, *Director of Communications*
Established in 1897

What/For Whom

The National PTA is a volunteer association that seeks to unite home, school, and community in promoting the education, health, and safety of children. Working through national, state, and local PTA associations, the organization is active in child advocacy causes. These include securing child labor laws; supporting compulsory public education, including kindergarten; creating a national public health service and developing health, safety, and nutrition programs for children; promoting education for children with special needs; providing parenthood education; organizing and improving school libraries; and establishing a juvenile justice system. The association is also concerned with the issues of latchkey children, discipline, and parent and community involvement in education. Most PTA members are parents, but some are teachers, school administrators, students, senior citizens, and individuals with or without children.

Examples

1) The Big City PTA Project began in 1986 to strengthen urban PTAs and reach out to parents who have not been traditionally involved in their children's reading.

2) National PTA presents its Reading/Literacy Award to a local unit that has conducted an outstanding reading program. The award recognizes PTAs that have encouraged parents to help their children become readers, developed creative ways to increase an interest in reading by students, and hosted cooperative projects between schools and libraries.

3) National PTA is a reading promotion partner of the Center for the Book in the Library of Congress (§32).

Publications

PTA Today, the association's magazine, published seven times a year; *What's Happening in Washington,* a newsletter that keeps PTA members informed about pending federal legislation affecting children and youth; brochures on evaluating schools, juvenile justice systems, television, preschool development, and other subjects and other newsletters, reports, brochures, planning kits, and guides.

Sources of Support

Membership dues, sale of publications, proceeds from conventions, and foundation assistance.

---

§84   National Reading Conference (NRC)

11 East Hubbard, Suite 200
Chicago, IL 60611
312-329-2512
Fax: 312-329-9131
Judith C. Burnison, *Executive Director*
Founded in 1950

What/For Whom

The National Reading Conference is a nonprofit, professional organization whose members, including college and university professors, share an interest in research and dissemination of information on oral and written language and use. The NRC encourages the study of literacy problems at all educational levels, with special emphasis on college and adult literacy; stimulates and promotes research in developmental, corrective, and remedial reading and writing; and studies the factors that influence progress in reading and writing. The conference also assists in the development of teacher-training programs, disseminates knowledge helpful in the solution of problems related to reading, and holds an annual conference.

Examples

During the annual conference held the first week in December, the Oscar S. Causey Award is presented for outstanding contributions to reading research. Other awards presented include the Student Outstanding Research Award and the Albert J. Kingston Award for outstanding contributions to reading service.

Publications

JRB: Journal of Reading Behavior, a quarterly; the *NRC Yearbook*, a biannual newsletter; and research results.

Sources of Support

Membership dues and sale of publications.

---

§85 Newspaper Association of America Foundation (NAA Foundation)

The Newspaper Center
11600 Sunrise Valley Drive
Reston, VA 22091
703-648-1051
Fax: 703-620-1265
Betty L. Sullivan, *Director/Education Services*
Established in 1961

What/For Whom

The Newspaper Association of America Foundation (formerly American Newspaper Publishers Association Foundation) is a public nonprofit educational foundation devoted to encouraging the advancement of freedom of speech and the press. Its programs encompass four basic objectives: developing informed and intelligent newspaper readers; enhancing minority opportunity in newspaper work; developing and strengthening public understanding of a free press; and advancing the professionalism of the press.

Examples

1) The Newspaper in Education (NIE) program, a major NAA Foundation service, aids parents and educators in teaching young people the fundamentals of reading and of informed citizenship. The NIE program is a cooperative effort between daily newspapers and thousands of U.S. and Canadian schools that use the newspapers to teach a variety of subjects: social studies, math, history, and English, as well as reading. The NAA Foundation is a coordinating agency for these local programs. It develops and distributes materials, sponsors conferences for developing NIE programs, and advises individual schools and newspapers. The newspapers themselves provide copies of

their papers to schools at discount prices, offer curriculum materials and teacher training, and generally help schools develop newspaper use for student learning.

National NIE Week, annually cosponsored by the International Reading Association (§61) and the NAA Foundation in cooperation with state and regional press associations, promotes the teaching of reading in the classroom through the use of newspapers.

2) The NAA Foundation is a sponsoring member of the First Amendment Congress, a coalition of sixteen media organizations dedicated to enhancing America's awareness of the importance of freedom of expression in a democratic society. The NAA acts as the administrative service arm of the congress and publishes its newsletter. It also awards grants to support groups such as the Reporters Committee for Freedom of the Press and the World Press Freedom Committee.

3) Family Focus, an intergenerational literacy program launched in 1988, is cosponsored by the NAA Foundation, the American Association of School Administrators, the International Reading Association, the National Association of Elementary School Principals, the National Association of Secondary School Principals, the National Congress of Parents and Teachers (see §83), and the National Middle School Association. The program is designed to help parents use the newspaper with their children to promote reading and communication skills.

4) Press to Read. Through this program, the NAA Foundation encourages and assists newspapers in the development of adult literacy programs. The foundation has produced *Newspapers Meet the Challenge* (a handbook), *Showcase of Newspaper Literacy* (a review of some newspaper projects across the country), and a twenty-minute slide/video program about illiteracy. Literacy Creators workshops have also been conducted. The outreach program is aimed at developing cooperative projects with major educational organizations.

5) Family Reading Challenge, a joint project of NAA Foundation, the National Newspaper Association, the National Newspaper Publishers Association, and others encourages children to read the newspaper during the summer and culminates with local activities on or near September 8, International Literacy Day.

6) The NAA Foundation is a member of the National Coalition for Literacy (§75).

7) The NAA Foundation is a reading promotion partner of the Center for the Book in the Library of Congress (§32).

Publications

The NAA Foundation offers a variety of materials for newspapers and subsequently by teachers in the classroom in the following major areas: the Newspaper in Education program, career education, support of the First Amendment, furthering work force diversity in the newspaper business and promoting literacy; *Update NIE*, a quarterly report; and *Press to Read*, the literacy newsletter issued five times during the year to newspaper publishers, editors, and others interested in literacy news.

Sources of Support

NAA Foundation programs and publications income; sale of promotional material; and proceeds from the foundation's endowment fund, which is supported by contributions from newspapers, newspaper organizations, and individuals in the newspaper business.

---

§86 OPAM America, Inc.

1714 Amwell Road, P.O. Box 5657
Somerset, NJ 08875-5657
908-297-9090
Fax: 908-297-6799
Rev. John Bertello, IMC, *National Director*
OPAM founded in 1972; OPAM America established in 1985

What/For Whom

OPAM America is an affiliate of OPAM, an international organization whose purpose is to combat illiteracy throughout the world and foster basic education. OPAM is an acronym for the original Italian name "Opera di Promozione della Alfabetizzazione nel Mondo," or Organization for the Promotion of World Literacy. OPAM expands the accepted definition of illiterate person as one who does not know how to read, write, or compute mathematically to include one who is also ignorant of any and all of those aspects of life which contribute to the benefit and development of the person, community, society, and country. OPAM promotes community development especially in developing countries through centers for literacy, schools of agronomy and crafts, professional technical instruction, domestic science and hygiene schools, and centers for women's development. OPAM operates by providing resources—money, tools, books—to groups already operating in the field, mostly missionaries. Founded by Msgr. Carlo Muratore, OPAM provides support not only to Catholic missionaries but to Protestant missionaries and others as well. OPAM America educates Americans about the extent of world illiteracy and its results and raises funds for literacy projects. OPAM chapters have been established in Pennsylvania and California to support OPAM through fund raising activities.

Publications

OPAM America for world literacy, quarterly newsletter.

| Sources of Support | Tax-deductible contributions from individuals, organizations, foundations, and institutions and annual membership pledges. |

---

§87   PEN American Center

568 Broadway
New York, NY 10012
212-334-1660
Fax: 212-334-2181
John Morrone, *Programs and Publications*
Established in 1921

What/For Whom

PEN American Center is the largest of more than eighty centers that make up PEN International, founded in London by John Galsworthy to foster understanding among men and women of letters in all countries. Members of PEN work for freedom of expression wherever it has been endangered. International PEN is the only worldwide organization of writers and a chief voice of the literary community. The membership of PEN American Center includes poets, playwrights, editors, essayists, novelists, translators, and those editors and agents who have made a substantial contribution to the literary community. Membership is by invitation. PEN's activities include public literary events, conferences, international congresses, literary awards, and assistance to writers in prison and to American writers in financial need.

Examples

1) Freedom-to-Write, working on behalf of approximately eighty writers in forty countries each year, is actively engaged in protesting the harassment of writers worldwide with letter and cable campaigns, missions by American authors to foreign countries, press releases and press conferences, public events, case sheets, country reports, and monthly bulletins. It fights book-banning in libraries and schools around the United States and offers testimony in Congress on issues affecting writers.

2) The Prison Writing Program administers an annual writing competition for incarcerated writers and provides information and referrals to inmates about writing and publishing.

3) The Children's Book Authors' Committee sponsors regular public events focusing on the art of writing for children and young adults and on the diversity of literature for juvenile readers.

4) The PEN Reading Program encourages Americans to read literature more regularly, more critically, and more adventurously by sending writers to public schools, commu-

nity centers, and libraries to discuss a particular book as well as issues pertaining to writing and culture.

5) Among the awards PEN gives are the Ernest Hemingway Foundation Award for first novels and the PEN/Faulkner Award for fiction.

Publications

PEN Newsletter, a quarterly; *Freedom-to-Write Bulletin,* published irregularly; *Grants and Awards Available to American Writers,* a biennial directory; and many reports, pamphlets, and books.

Sources of Support

Sale of publications and videotapes; contributions from individuals, corporations, and foundations.

---

§88   Poets & Writers, Inc.

72 Spring Street
New York, NY 10012
212-226-3586
Fax: 212-226-3963
Elliot Figman, *Director*
Established in 1970

What/For Whom

Poets & Writers, Inc., is a nonprofit service organization for the United States literary community. It publishes materials on practical topics related to writing, such as copyright, literary agents, literary bookstores, workshop sponsors, grants, and taxes. It helps pay writers' fees for public readings and workshops in New York state and provides assistance to groups wishing to start such programs. It supplies addresses, facts, and referrals of interest to the writing community nationwide. It provides its services through four programs: Publications, Information Center, Readings/Workshops, and Writers Exchange.

Examples

1) The Readings/Workshops Program develops audiences for contemporary literature and helps writers survive financially by paying fees to writers who give readings or workshops sponsored by groups in New York state and several other states.

2) The Information Center will supply free of charge, over the telephone, facts or information about the professional side of writers' lives, provide writers' current addresses, and answer questions relating to writers' practical needs.

Publications

Poets & Writers Magazine, published six times a year, provides practical news and comments on publishing, jobs, grants, taxes, and other topics. Also, reference books, sourcebooks, and guides.

Sources of Support

Grants from the Literature Program of the National Endowment for the Arts (§79) and the Literature Program of the New York State Council on the Arts and the New York City Department of Cultural Affairs and contributions from corporations, foundations, and individuals.

---

§89 Printing Industries of America, Inc. (PIA)

100 Daingerfield Road
Alexandria, VA 22314
703-519-8100
Fax: 703-548-3227
Ray Roper, *Executive Director*
Established 1887

What/For Whom

Printing Industries of America, Inc. is the world's largest graphic arts trade association, serves more than thirteen thousand member firms. Through a network of over thirty local affiliates in the United States and Canada and special industry groups, PIA provides service in the areas of government relations, environmental issues, sales and marketing, human resources, and management education. Services cover a wide spectrum of benefits including publications, meetings, products, regulatory and legislative information and representation, and industrial relations consulting.

Example

The Binding Industries of America, one of the special industry groups, represents trade binders and looseleaf manufacturers with newsletters, bulletins, surveys, phone consultation, management referral services, a product competition, and an annual convention.

Publications

Each service area has its own publications and all publications are featured in the *PIA Bookstore Catalog.*

Sources of Support

Membership fees and sale of publications.

§90 Project Learning U.S. (PLUS)

4802 Fifth Avenue
Pittsburgh, PA 15213
412-622-1492
Margot Woodwell, *PBS Project Director*
John E. Harr, *ABC Project Director*
Established in 1985

What/For Whom

Project Learning U.S. (PLUS), a joint national public service campaign of Capital Cities/ABC, Inc., and the Public Broadcasting Service (PBS), was established to combine local community efforts with a national media focus on combatting the problem of adult literacy in the United States. Originally known as Project Literacy U.S., PLUS's goals were to raise national awareness of the problem of adult functional illiteracy in America, to develop and encourage volunteer action to address illiteracy, and to encourage those who need help to participate. PLUS, redesignated Project Learning U.S. in 1992, now has a broader focus on general education issues, emphasizing the fact that lifelong learning incorporates all learning and that literacy is far more that just reading.

Both ABC and PBS provide on-air national coverage of the illiteracy problem in all varieties of news and informational programming as well as public service announcements. PLUS has a membership of more than 150 national support organizations drawn from broadcasters and literacy service providers and a broad-based coalition of community leaders which form the Public Television Outreach Alliance made up of more than 550 local task forces.

Examples

1) Public service announcements form the backbone of the PLUS commitment to exposure to literacy and education issues, an ongoing presence bridging special PLUS events and programs. Capital Cities/ABC is committed to a full weekly schedule of PLUS PSAs on the ABC television network throughout the day making PLUS the most widely distributed public service campaign from a single source in media history.

2) PLUS is a partner with the Institute for the Study of Adult Literacy (§55), WQED/Pittsburgh, and WPSX/Penn State in Project Lifelong Learning, a major initiative to improve adult literacy and lifelong learning programs in the workplace, in the community, and in the family.

3) In 1986, PLUS established READAmerica, a nonprofit reading advocacy foundation whose national programs partner with other organizations. For the READ, America! Summer program, a three-year campaign begun in 1993 to promote intergenerational reading, partners with READAmerica include the American Association for Retired Persons (§5), American Library Association (§12), and National PTA (§83).

110

4) PLUS is a member of the National Coalition for Literacy (§75).

5) PLUS is a reading promotion partner of the Center for the Book in the Library of Congress (§32).

Publications   PLUS quarterly newsletter and monthly update and a PLUS directory of contact people.

Source of Support   Contributions from corporations.

---

§91   Publishers Marketing Association (PMA)

2401 Pacific Coast Highway, Suite 102
Hermosa Beach, CA 90254
310-372-2732
Fax: 310-374-3342
Jan Nathan, *Executive Director*
Established in 1983

What/For Whom   Publishers Marketing Association is a nonprofit trade association of more than twelve hundred members representing independent book, audio, video, and specialty publishers throughout the United States and Canada. The association advances the interests of these publishers by offering cooperative marketing programs and publications and acting as an advocate for the publishing industry. PMA conducts a major seminar before the American Booksellers Association (§7) convention and holds other seminars and ongoing marketing programs around the country during the year. The association also administers an awards program and exhibits at major book shows.

Examples   1) PMA's annual Publishing University Program is a two-day series of seminars on all aspects of publishing held for its members before the ABA convention and trade show. Member publishers are given the opportunity to exchange vital information and to gain education on editorial, graphics, marketing, and budgeting and forecasting issues.

2) PMA honors independent publishing excellence with the Benjamin Franklin Awards competition. Publishers compete with each other in specific genres, as well as various design categories.

Publications   *PMA Newsletter*, a monthly, and a membership directory.

Sources of Support   Membership dues.

§92 PUBWATCH

35 West 67th Street
New York, NY 10023
212-362-4618
Fax: 212-362-5011
Peter B. Kaufman, *Director*
Established in 1990

What/For Whom

PUBWATCH is a nonprofit organization that promotes and coordinates Western assistance to book publishers and booksellers in Central and Eastern Europe, the Baltic countries, and the Commonwealth of Independent States. PUBWATCH works with several organizations, including the American Booksellers Association (§7), the Association of University Presses (§20), the British Publishers Association, and the Soros Foundation to bring assistance programs to these regions. These educational and informational programs include demonstration seminars on publishing in a market economy, workshops on printing and distribution reform, schools for booksellers, and publishing resource centers.

Examples

1) PUBWATCH and the American Booksellers Association cosponsored professional bookseller training schools in Budapest, Bratislava, and Warsaw, which provided participants with insight on how to run a retail trade store.

2) PUBWATCH and the Association of American University Presses cosponsored workshops on "Scholarly Publishing in a Market Economy" in Estonia and Czechoslovakia.

3) PUBWATCH with the Center for the Book in the Library of Congress (§32) and the Kennan Institute for Advanced Studies sponsored a conference in March 1993 on "Publishing and Book Culture in Russia and the New States: Opportunities for the West."

Publications

PUBWATCH Update, issued quarterly, announces new programs of aid available to publishers and booksellers in Central and Eastern Europe; also, the *1992 Directory of Western Organizations Assisting Book Culture in Central and Eastern Europe and The Commonwealth of Independent States.*

Sources of Support

Grants and contributions from corporations and individuals.

§93   Push Literacy Action Now (PLAN)

1332 G Street, SE
Washington, DC 20003
202-547-8903
Catherine Baker, *Executive Director*
Established in 1972

What/For Whom

Push Literacy Action Now is a nonprofit, community-based, literacy program whose mission is to meet the literacy and human development needs of low-literate adults and their families and to challenge the conditions that cause and perpetuate illiteracy. Primarily a volunteer organization, PLAN serves the community of the District of Columbia and also addresses literacy problems on a national scale by providing tutoring, testing, information and referral services, teacher training, and advocacy. PLAN emphasizes small-group classes. Instruction is provided to individuals in-house and to local companies in the workplace. The focus is on adults reading below the sixth-grade level.

PLAN's program emphasizes the need for changes in the society that surrounds those who cannot read. PLAN advocates acceptance of new regulations governing the readability of printed matter for the general public and teaches workshops in writing and analyzing welfare and school reports, manuals, legal and insurance documents, and other communications to promote more widespread readability. PLAN also urges that literacy be regarded as a basic rather than a support service. To attract greater numbers of people to literacy instruction, for example, PLAN believes that it will be necessary to provide them with support services such as transportation and child care.

Examples

1) Take Up Reading Now (TURN) is designed to bring attention to the needs of low-literate, low-income parents and their children. This program has three parts: Take PART (Parents As Reading Teachers) includes public awareness activities and special training for low-literate parents of children age six months to two years; Take CARE (Child Advocacy for Reading Education) offers support to parents of children in lower grades; and Take a BOOK is a "one-way, take-a-book" library for at-risk children living in low-income neighborhoods.

2) Through the Just Say It! campaign, PLAN works with public and private service agencies to teach them to produce documents that are not only easier to read for the average consumer, but also accessible to readers with more limited literacy skills.

Publications

The Ladder, a bimonthly newsletter distributed nationally, provides commentary on literacy issues. *Laying the Foundations:*

113

A Parent/Child Literacy Training Kit is designed to help professionals who seek to create or extend family literacy programs by providing theory and practical ideas plus sample materials. Also, *From the Crib to the Classroom,* a twelve-minute video for parents and *A Look at Illiteracy in America Today: The Problem, the Solutions, the Alternatives,* a position paper which takes a critical look at the adult literacy effort in the United States and provides suggestions for change.

Sources of Support Contributions from foundations, community groups, corporations, and individuals and minimal tuition fees paid by students.

---

§94   Reading Is Fundamental, Inc. (RIF)

600 Maryland Avenue, SW, Suite 600
Washington, DC 20024
202-287-3220
Fax: 202-287-3196
Ruth Graves, *President*
Anne Richardson, *Board Chair*
Established in 1966

What/For Whom Reading Is Fundamental (RIF is a private, nonprofit, nationwide organization affiliated with the Smithsonian Institution. Founded by Margaret S. McNamara as a single neighborhood pilot project, RIF reaches children in over fifty states, Puerto Rico, the U.S. Virgin Islands, and Guam by ensuring that they have books in their homes; providing activities to stimulate reading interest; making it possible for children to choose and own books; encouraging reading for pleasure; and involving parents in their children's reading.

The national RIF organization has helped start RIF projects in schools, libraries, hospitals, day-care centers, correctional facilities, and migrant farmworker communities. The projects are run largely by a grassroots network of more than 140,000 volunteers and involve parents, educators, librarians, and business and civic leaders. RIF projects include book distributions, festive occasions when youngsters select and keep books that they like, and reading-related activities at the grassroots level, for example, dramatic skits, poster and essay contests, and talks on reading by athletes and entertainers. RIF provides local volunteers with guidance materials, workshops, special discounts and services from book suppliers, information on reading motivation techniques. In addition, RIF mounts an ongoing national campaign to promote children's literacy, conducts two national contests to celebrate children and reading, and develops innovative programs to meet the special needs of target populations.

Examples

1) Reading Is Fun Week is an annual nationwide celebration of reading highlighted by the presentation of the In Celebration of Reading Award to the National RIF Reader and acknowledgment of RIF's National Poster Contest winner. The celebration program is designed to encourage youngsters to read, outside of school hours, books unconnected with school assignments.

2) Family of Readers is a program which provides guidelines and techniques to involve adult learners or parents in running the RIF program for their children.

3) The Shared Beginnings program offers teen parents skills that will enable them to nurture their children while they take an active role in developing their children's preliteracy skills.

4) RIF is a reading promotion partner of the Center for the Book in the Library of Congress (§32).

Publications

RIF Newsletter, a quarterly; *The RIF Guide to Encouraging Young Readers*, descriptions of 200 reading-related activities for parents and children with recommendations of popular books and resources; the *Parent Guide Brochures* series of low-cost pamphlets covering a variety of topics related to families and reading; *A Guide to RIF's Family Literacy Programs*; booklets and instructional pamphlets; and posters and bookmarks. A complete listing of RIF publications is available upon request.

Sources of Support

Contributions from individuals, corporations, foundations, and a government contract that enables national RIF to help local RIF projects pay for books.

§95 Reading Rainbow

601 West 50th Street-Penthouse
New York, NY 10019
212-977-9100
Fax: 212-977-9164
Laura M. Frame, *Publicity Director*
Established in 1983

What/For Whom

Reading Rainbow is a PBS television series designed to motivate children to read on their own for pleasure and entertainment and to see books as part of their everyday lives. The productions mark one of the first collaborations of the publishing and television worlds to promote reading by young viewers coast to coast. Hosted by actor LeVar Burton, the series has a half-hour video magazine format that features an adaptation of a children's book followed by on-location "real life" situations and book reviews by children reviewers. Celebrity narrators featured on the show include Jason Robards, Ruby Dee, Bill Cosby, Roy Clark, and Jane Curtin. Other features include animation, music videos, dances, songs, and "kid on the street" interviews.

The Association for Library Service to Children, a division of the American Library Association (§12), served on the project's advisory council with the National PTA (§83), the Association for Supervision and Curriculum Development, and the International Reading Association (§61). The series is a production of Great Plains National/Nebraska Educational TV Network/and WNED-TV, Buffalo, and is produced by Lancit Media Productions, Ltd., in New York.

Examples

1) An episode during the tenth-anniversary season featured the book *Sam and the Sea Cow* by Francine Jacobs and illustrated by Laura Kelly. LeVar traveled to Sea World in Florida for an up-close look at these gentle giants in their natural habitat.

2) In 1986, Reading Rainbow featured science programming for the first time with grants underwritten by the Carnegie Corporation of New York and the National Science Foundation.

3) Reading Rainbow, in partnership with the productions Long Ago & Far Away and Wonderworks, has formed the Family Literacy Alliance to encourage public television stations to bring the joy and fun of reading to families by reaching new audiences for the three shows and PBS stations. The alliance also works with local agencies and organizations to find ways of integrating the shows into existing community programs and to be a resource for those agencies by making available broadcast schedules and access to tapes of the three productions.

Publications

Reading Rainbow Teacher Guides summarize each program and provide discussion topics, related activities, and supplemental booklists. *Science Guides* feature the season's science programs. *Reading Rainbow Library* is a set of ten books featured on the show that also include games and behind-the-scenes and related program activities. Individual Reading Rainbow videocassettes are available for educational use, as are Reading Rainbow songs on audiocassettes.

Sources of Support

Funding from the Kellogg Company, the Corporation for Public Broadcasting, the National Science Foundation, and public television viewers.

§96   Reading Reform Foundation

P.O. Box 98785
Tacoma, WA 98498-0785
206-588-3436
Marian A. Hinds, *President*
Established in 1961

What/For Whom

The Reading Reform Foundation is a national nonprofit educational organization committed to restoring literacy "by returning the alphabet, phonics first, to the teaching of reading." The membership believes that almost every child, regardless of social and economic background, can learn to read, write, and spell if taught by effective methods. The foundation also focuses on intensive phonics for older students and adults, disseminates information on the reading crisis and phonetics through local support groups; sponsors workshops and an annual conference; offers referral services, including a literacy clearinghouse and technical assistance to remedial reading programs; and gives testimony before groups.

Examples

1) Reading Reform Foundation of New York offers workshops for parents aimed primarily at getting children ready to learn to read. These courses also include some tips for helping older children with schoolwork.

2) RRF offers courses and or workshops for teachers and others desiring to learn how to teach phonics.

Publications

The Sounds of Reading, published irregularly; and various manuals, reports, video cassettes, booklets, and articles.

Sources of Support

Membership dues, sale of publications, and donations, grants from foundations, and individual contributions.

§97   Small Press Center

20 West 44th Street
New York, NY 10036
212-764-7021
Karin Taylor, *Director*
Founded in 1984

What/For Whom

Small Press Center is a nonprofit organization dedicated to promoting interaction between the public and small independent book publishers. The center promotes books by independent publishers, helps to make the public more aware of small press titles, and provides a place for people to order them.

117

Membership enables small press publishers to draw upon many services including free shelf space in the center's library, free listing in the annual catalog, a month-long exhibit in the display window at the center's facilities, and the availability of a reception and book reading facility for introduction of new titles.

Example

The center sponsors an annual Small Press book fair that provides publishers with direct access to the reading public, lunchtime readings, broadcasts, receptions, special exhibits, and other programs to stimulate public interest in small press publications.

Publications

SPC Newsletter and the *Small Press Center Directory*, an annual catalog of books by small press publishers that is distributed to book buyers at major public and academic libraries and nationwide to independent book stores.

Sources of Support

Contributions, membership dues, grants, and sponsorship by the General Society Library, where the center is housed.

---

§98   Society for Scholarly Publishing (SSP)

10200 West 44th Avenue, Suite 304
Wheat Ridge, CO 80033
303-422-3914
Fax: 303-422-8894
Francine Butler, *Executive Director*
Founded in 1979

What/For Whom

The Society for Scholarly Publishing is a national organization serving the scholarly publishing community as a whole. Its membership includes university presses, for-profit scholarly and professional presses, professional associations, museums, reference and database publishers, printers, individuals who work in these areas, librarians, and other information professionals. The society provides for communication among these professionals, gives educational seminars, and in general helps its members to keep abreast of publishing trends, both technological and managerial. SSP holds an annual meeting in addition to its seminars and workshops.

Example

"Marketing and Distribution of Scholarly Publications" is a day-and-a-half-long SSP seminar covering such topics as planning, marketing online services, and marketing books and journals.

Publications   *Scholarly Publishing Today*, a newsletter published six times a year, carries SSP news, special reports, and regular columns; *Scholarly Publishing*, a quarterly; and a directory of members.

Sources of Support   Membership fees, grants from foundations, and revenues from meetings and seminars.

---

§99 Society of Children's Book Writers and Illustrators (SCBWI)

22736 Vanoween Street, Suite 106
West Hills, CA 91307
818-888-8760
Lin Oliver, *Executive Director*
Established in 1968

What/For Whom   The Society of Children's Book Writers and Illustrators is a professional organization for writers and illustrators of children's literature that offers a variety of services to people who write, illustrate, or share a vital interest in children's literature. SCBWI acts as a network for the exchange of information among children's writers, illustrators, editors, publishers, agents, librarians, educators, bookstore personnel, and others involved with literature for young people.

Examples   1) SCBWI annually sponsors a national conference devoted entirely to writing and illustrating literature for children.

2) The society administers a free manuscript exchange so that SCBWI members can obtain professional criticism and reaction to their works in progress.

3) SCBWI awards Golden Kite statuettes each year for excellence in the field of children's books and presents magazine merit awards for outstanding original magazine work for young people during that year written or illustrated by SCBWI members.

Publications   *SCBWI Bulletin*, a bimonthly containing comprehensive and current information in the field of children's literature, and occasional monographs.

Source of Support   Membership dues.

119

§100 Special Libraries Association (SLA)

1700 18th Street, NW
Washington, DC 20009-2508
202-234-4700
Fax: 202-265-9317
Mark Serepca, *Director of Communications*
Founded in 1909

What/For Whom

Special Libraries Association is a nonprofit, international professional organization of more than 13,500 members who work in special libraries serving corporate, research, government, technical, and academic institutions that use or produce specialized information. The primary goal of the association is to advance the leadership role of the special librarian or information professional by providing a variety of services to enhance members' professional skills and advance the interests of the special libraries community. SLA is made up of fifty-five regional chapters, twenty-seven subject divisions, and numerous committees. The association holds an annual conference and other meetings; conducts continuing education programs; administers scholarships, grants, and awards; and provides other services of benefit to its membership.

Examples

1) The chapters, as the regional units of SLA, have meetings often featuring guest speakers, professional events, or special social activities. For example, the Eastern Canada chapter used their holiday social to raise money for the Kenya library book fund, and the Southern California chapter sponsored a "Save the Books" dinner for the fire-ravaged Los Angeles Public Library.

2) The divisions serve members' technical and subject interests through educational programs, publications, and cooperative projects with other information-related organizations. SLA divisions include advertising and marketing, business and finance, education, engineering, environmental and resource management, library management, metals/materials, military librarians, museums/arts and humanities, newspapers, nuclear science, solo librarians, and telecommunications.

3) SLA is a reading promotion partner of the Center for the Book in the Library of Congress (§32).

Publications

Specialist, a monthly newsletter with association news and reports on events taking place in the information community and current developments in the field; *Special Libraries*, a quarterly scholarly journal; *Who's Who in Special Libraries*, the annual membership directory; and numerous monographs and pamphlets. Each chapter publishes its own newsletter and the divisions also produce books and other publications that address a variety of specialized topics.

Sources of Support   Membership dues, contributions from foundations and corporations, and sale of publications.

---

§101   Syndicated Fiction Project

P.O. Box 15650
Washington, DC 20003
202-543-6322
Caroline Marshall, *Project Director*
Created in 1982

What/For Whom   The Syndicated Fiction Project was created by the National Endowment for the Arts (§79) to revive the custom of newspapers carrying fiction, a practice that increased the audience for literature in the late nineteen- and early twentieth centuries. The project invites anyone interested in writing short stories—both famous and fresh, new talents—to submit their stories each January for consideration by writers whose own work is highly regarded. As a result of selection, authors receive an initial monetary award for the right to circulate their work to participating magazines and newspapers and to make an audio recording of their story. The winner receives an additional monetary award each time the story appears in print.

Examples   1) From 1982 to 1991, more than 475 stories were published by twenty-eight newspapers in their Sunday magazines and feature sections.

2) Award-winning works become eligible for the Project's "Annual Best." Under this program three authors are invited to perform at a celebratory reading in Washington. Several of these readings have been held in cooperation with the Library of Congress Poetry and Literature Center (see §64).

3) In 1987, the radio "story hour" was resurrected. Stories syndicated through this market and the newspapers reach a combined potential of ten million people on "The Sound of Writing," a half-hour show which is aired on National Public Radio stations.

Publications   *The Sound of Writing: America's Short Story Magazine on the Air.*

Sources of Support   National Public Radio, grants from the National Endowment for the Arts, other gifts, and user fees.

§102 Teachers & Writers Collaborative (T&W)

5 Union Square West
New York, NY 10003-3306
212-691-6590
Fax: 212-675-0171
Nancy Larson Shapiro, *Executive Director*
Established 1967

What/For Whom

Teachers & Writers Collaborative is a nonprofit organization that sends writers and artists into school and community settings to work with students and teachers. It also publishes innovative materials about teaching and writing that are distributed to a national audience. T&W serves as a national literary arts program, a book and magazine publisher, a distributor of creative educational materials, a writer-in-residency program, a community group that shares resources, and an adviser to other arts-in-education groups. The collaborative also conducts writing workshops.

Examples

1) The Muriel Rukeyser Workshops give established writers, whose commitments or locations prevent them from working with T&W over an extended period, an opportunity to learn about and participate in T&W programs. As guests in the classrooms of other writers in the program, they contribute to the students' experience of writing and exchange ideas about writing and teaching writing with the host writer.

2) T&W is home to the Center for Imaginative Writing, a library and meeting place for writers and educators.

3) T&W is a reading promotion partner of the Center for the Book in the Library of Congress (§32).

Publications

Teachers & Writers Magazine, a bimonthly; *Playmaking: Children Writing and Performing Their Own Plays*; and other books and games.

Sources of Support

Membership dues and contributions and grants from the New York State Council on the Arts and the National Endowment for the Arts (§79).

§103 U.S. Department of Commerce

202-482-6090
Washington, DC 20230

What/For Whom

Four agencies within the Department of Commerce are involved in programs of particular interest to the book community.

1) Through its **Bureau of Census** and other agencies, the Department of Commerce keeps statistics on United States publishing and the reading public. The department notes, "The nation's concern with improving reading and educational skills should help the U.S. book industry. . . . As the country's economy shifts toward services and away from goods production, the educational requirements of the workforce take on increased importance." Statistics on newspapers, periodicals, and books trace present and projected developments in the areas of printing, publishing, graphic arts, labor and material costs, advertising, and sales.

2) The **International Trade Administration** (ITA) was established in January 1980 to promote world trade and to strengthen the international trade and investment position of the United States. Its functions include (a) export promotion—trade exhibits, trade missions, catalog and video displays, and the rental of overseas trade centers; (b) formation of trade policy—including the protection of U.S. intellectual property overseas, and (c) trade analysis—studies of trade barriers, publication of trade data, and preparation of the annual *U.S. Industrial Outlook*, which consists of economic reviews and forecasts on the U.S. book publishing industry. Contact William S. Lofquist, Industry Specialist, International Trade Administration—Printing and Publishing, at 202-482-0379.

3) The **National Institute of Standards and Technology** (formerly National Bureau of Standards) supplies the measurement foundation for U.S. industry science and technology. Since 1979, the bureau has trained librarians from developing countries in technical and scientific librarianship. For additional information, contact the Information Resources and Services Division at 301-975-3058.

4) The **National Technical Information Service** (NTIS) is the central source for the public sale and distribution of government-sponsored research, development and engineering reports, foreign technical reports, and reports prepared by local government agencies. Periodicals data-base files, computer programs, and U.S. government-owned patent applications are also available. Anyone may search the NTIS Biblio-

graphic Data online, using the services of organizations that maintain the data-base for public use through contractual relationships with NTIS. The agency is self-supporting in that all costs of its products and services are paid from sales income. For additional information, contact the NTIS Office of Customer Services at 703-487-4660.

Publications

Census of Manufactures, Annual Survey of Manufactures, and *County Business Patterns,* published on a periodic basis by the Bureau of the Census, contain extensive statistics on U.S. book publishing (statistically classified as industry 2731). The *U.S. Industrial Outlook,* published annually by the International Trade Administration, contains economic analyses and projections on the book publishing industry. Full summaries of current U.S. and foreign research reports are published regularly by NTIS in a wide variety of weekly newsletters, a biweekly journal, an annual index, and various subscription formats.

Source of Support

Federal government.

---

§104 U.S. Department of Education

400 Maryland Avenue, SW
Washington, DC 20202
202-401-1576

What/For Whom

The Department of Education establishes policies for administrators and coordinates most federal assistance to education. The secretary of education advises the president on education plans, policies, and programs of the federal government. The secretary directs department staff in carrying out the approved activities and promotes public understanding of the department's objectives and programs. Several offices and divisions within the Department of Education conduct programs of special interest to the book community. The department is a member of the National Coalition for Literacy (§75) and a reading promotion partner of the Center for the Book in the Library of Congress (§32).

Examples

1) **The Office of Vocational and Adult Education (OVAE), Division of Adult Education and Literacy**, administers the Adult Education Act, under which basic grants to states are made—the major program supporting services for educationally disadvantaged adults. The division also administers discretionary grant programs for workplace literacy and education for homeless adults. It operates a clearinghouse for information resources in adult education and literacy; publishes a

bimonthly newsletter, the *A.L.L. Points Bulletin*; and reports on promising practices and trends in adult education. For additional information, call 202-205-8270.

Following are descriptions of the major programs administered by OVAE.

The state-administered grant program is the major source of federal support for educating adults over age sixteen who are not currently enrolled in school, lack a high school diploma, or lack the basic skills to function at work or in their daily lives. Programs of instruction include adult basic education, adult secondary education, and English as a second language.

The **National Workplace Literacy Program** provides financial support for demonstration projects that teach literacy and other skills needed in the workplace. Projects funded are selected competitively and are operated by partnerships involving local business, industry, labor organizations or private industry councils, and education agencies.

Through the **Adult Literacy Program for the Homeless**, grants are issued competitively every five years for projects that help the homeless develop basic education skills and the self-esteem needed to move beyond basic survival needs.

The **State Literacy Resource Center Program**, authorized by the National Literacy Act of 1991, provides for establishment of an adult literacy resource center in each state or region. These centers are part of a network of information sources that includes the Department of Education and the National Institute for Literacy (§82). The centers are designed to facilitate delivery of education services to adults by multiple providers in the field.

2) **Education Resources Information Center** (ERIC), established in 1966 and located in the Office of Educational Research and Improvement (OERI), is a national system that collects and disseminates findings of research and development and descriptions of exemplary programs in various education fields. It is a major data-base center for fugitive information on reading, English, speech, journalism, theater, and related communication fields. ERIC clearinghouses are operated under federal contracts by education organizations and institutions around the country. (For an example, see §30.) The clearinghouses or centers collect, evaluate, abstract, and index hard-to-find educational literature; conduct computer searches; commission studies; and act as resource guides. The information collected is listed in the network's reference publications and indexed in extensive computerized files. Each of the sixteen clearinghouses or centers is responsible for a particular educational area. More than seven hundred educational institutions, roughly one-tenth of them

abroad, carry the entire ERIC collection and make it available to the public.

The ERIC Review, published three times a year by ACCESS ERIC, announces research results, publications, and new programs as well as information on programs, research, publications, and services of ERIC. *Resources in Education (RIE),* a monthly reference journal, contains abstracts of each educational item that ERIC collects and makes available to current educational periodicals containing ERIC annotations of journal articles. For more information about ERIC, call ACCESS ERIC toll free at 1-800-USE-ERIC.

3) **Library Programs**, established in 1985 in the Office of Educational Research and Improvement, administers a variety of programs authorized by the Library Services and Construction Act (LSCA) and the Higher Education Act (HEA). Library Programs' support is used to provide seed money for innovative or experimental programs, assist literacy projects, encourage the development of services to disadvantaged populations, provide financial incentives to libraries to share resources, and conduct evaluations and research on library issues. For additional information, call 202-219-2293.

4) The **National Center for Educational Statistics** gathers, analyzes, and synthesizes data on the characteristics and performance of American education. The areas covered include public and nonpublic elementary and secondary education; postsecondary education, including college and university libraries; and vocational and adult education. The center is located within the Office of Educational Research and Improvement (OERI). For additional information, call 202-219-1828.

5) The **Office of Bilingual Education** works for equal educational opportunity and improved programs for "limited proficiency and minority languages populations" by providing support for programs, activities, and management initiatives that meet their special needs for bilingual education. The office administers the Family English Literacy Grants which provide limited-English-proficient families, adults, and out-of-school youth with instruction in the English language. For further information, call 202-205-8728.

6) The **Office of Research (OR)** supports the scholarly and academic work of individuals and institutions. The research is designed to advance knowledge about educational practice and is aimed at solving or alleviating specific educational problems. OR supports the educational research and development centers which have been established to conduct research in several areas including teaching, learning, teacher education, writing, and reading. The Reading Research and Education Center (see §33) is one example.

Source of Support   Federal government.

§105   U.S. Information Agency (USIA)

301 Fourth Street, SW
Washington, DC 20547
202-619-4355

What/For Whom

The United States Information Agency is responsible for the government's overseas educational and cultural programs. Several of its activities are of particular concern to the book community, including the USIA library, book export, translation, exhibits, and book donation programs. For information, call the Office of Cultural Centers and Resources at 202-619-4866.

Examples

1) USIA maintains close to 160 libraries and reading rooms in almost one hundred countries. The agency also provides support for library programs in binational centers in more than twenty countries. The focus of these collections is on materials that will help people in foreign countries learn about the United States, its people, history, culture, and political and social processes. For further information, contact the Library Program Division at 202-619-4923.

2) The Book Program Division organizes exhibits of American books for major international book fairs. This division also promotes the dissemination of American books abroad, either through English reprints or by translation into some fifteen languages, and assembles exhibits of appropriate American publications for overseas professional events, seminars, libraries, and scholarly institutions. The division publishes *BOOKLINE*, which keeps field service officers informed of services available. For further information, call 202-619-4922.

3) The Library Fellows Program was initiated in 1986 with a USIA grant to the American Library Association (§12). The purpose of the program is to place American library and publishing professionals in foreign institutions or organizations for periods of several months to a year to carry out projects identified as important to U.S. and host-country interests. Projects include organizing a law collection, developing a school library, and compiling a list of U.S. books translated into Arabic. For further information, contact the program director at the American Library Association, 50 East Huron Street, Chicago, IL 60611; or call 800-545-2433, extension 3200 (fax: 312-944-3897).

4) The USIA is a reading promotion partner of the Center for the Book in the Library of Congress (§32).

Source of Support

Federal government.

§106   Western States Arts Federation (WESTAF)

236 Montezuma Avenue
Santa Fe, NM 87501
505-988-1166
Fax: 505-982-9307
Robert Sheldon, *Literature Coordinator*
Established in 1974

What/For Whom

The Western States Arts Federation is an association of twelve western state arts agencies that provide regional arts programs for their constituents in Alaska, Arizona, California, Colorado, Idaho, Montana, New Mexico, Oregon, Utah, Washington, and Wyoming. The federation's goal is to make excellence in the arts available to the people of the West and to promote the best of the region's arts to the rest of the nation. WESTAF combines artistic resources and professional activities to address a variety of important cultural needs and opportunities in the West. Programs include fellowships and exhibition opportunities in the visual arts, awards and promotional activities in literature, and a performing arts tour.

Example

The Western States Book Awards, established in 1984, is a biennial program recognizing excellence in creative nonfiction, fiction, and poetry from western writers and publishers.

Publications

WestWords, published irregularly; *WESTAF's National Arts Jobbank*, a biweekly newsletter; *On Board: Guiding Principles for Trustees of Not-For-Profit Organizations*; and other books of service to the arts community.

Sources of Support

Grants from the National Endowment for the Arts (§79) and gifts from corporations, foundations, and individuals.

§107   White House Conference on Library and Information Services Task Force (WHCLIST)

519 Windemere
Aberdeen, MD 21004
410-272-0708
Offie Clark, *President*
Founded in 1979

What/For Whom

The White House Conference on Library and Information Services Task Force was established as the result of a resolution adopted at the 1979 White House Conference on Libraries and Information Services. WHCLIST monitors the implementation of resolutions of the 1979 and 1991 White House conferences at the national and state levels, testifies at state and congressional hearings on relevant issues, and promotes citizen involvement in friends of libraries groups and other cultural organizations.

WHCLIST takes an active role in promoting literacy, books, and reading; helping to provide access to library and information services for all Americans; promoting the potential of technology for efficient and cost-effective delivery of library services; advocating increased library funding locally, statewide, and nationally; providing leadership for library issues; and planning for future library and information issues.

WHCLIST membership of more than seven hundred dues-paying members includes two delegates from each state and territory, one a professional and the other a lay delegate; the heads of state and territorial agencies; and individual corporate and organization members. In addition, six voting delegates are selected from each state to participate during the annual meeting.

Examples

1) WHCLIST annually compiles a *Report from the States* that details progress toward implementation of the White House conference resolutions. A national five-year review was prepared in 1984 and updated in 1985.

2) WHCLIST sponsors awards for excellence in several categories including the Outstanding Legislator, the Outstanding Citizen, and the Outstanding Publication of the year.

3) WHCLIST is a reading promotion partner of the Center for the Book in the Library of Congress (§32).

Publications

WHICLIST Reporter.

Sources of Support

Associate members' fees and contributions and grants.

§108 Women of the Evangelical Lutheran Church in America

8765 West Higgins Road
Chicago, IL 60631
312-380-2736
1-800-638-3522, extension 2736
Fax: 312-380-2419
Faith L. Fretheim, *Director for Literacy*

What/For Whom

The Women of the Evangelical Lutheran Church in America (ELCA), formerly Lutheran Church Women, support literacy under their Mission: Action programming. The Volunteer Reading Aides (VRA) Program was established in 1968 and is the nation's largest ecumenical literacy English-as-a-Second-Language project. VRA trains volunteer tutors, organizes community-based literacy programs where none exist, conducts literacy workshops for libraries and community agencies, and provides literacy referral and general information services to the church and the general public. Nonmembers of the Evangelical Lutheran Church of America are welcomed both as tutors and as students. Other literacy activities include an advocacy network and a public awareness campaign. Lutheran bookstores in eighteen cities have agreed to distribute several literacy titles produced by ELCA at low cost.

Examples

1) Through VRA, training is offered to professional teachers in the principles of teaching English to speakers of other languages (ESOL).

2) The VRA program has helped migrant and native Canadian groups select and write materials suited to specialized literacy needs.

Publications

The VRA program develops and publishes inexpensive, easy-to-read materials for new readers and ESOL students and resource materials for tutors and literacy program leaders.

Sources of Support

Donations from Women of the Evangelical Lutheran Church and other church members, sale of publications, films, and videotapes, and service fees from groups requesting assistance.

---

§109 Women's National Book Association (WNBA)

160 Fifth Avenue, Room 604
New York, NY 10010
212-675-7804
Sandra K. Paul, *Executive Director*
Founded in 1917

What/For Whom

The Women's National Book Association is a nonprofit professional association founded to give visibility to the role of women in the world of books and publishing, to bring together women and men active in the world of books, and to inform them as well as the general public about the need to create, produce, distribute and use books. WNBA is an umbrella organization, providing opportunity for book people to share ideas, information, and contacts. It sponsors awards for women in the book industry and for sellers of children's books. The association has active chapters in Binghamton,

Boston, Detroit, Los Angeles, Nashville, New York, San Francisco, and Washington.

Examples

1) The Women's National Book Association Award (formerly the Constance Lindsay Skinner Award) honors women in the book world who have made a difference in bringing authors and their readers together.

2) The Lucile Micheels Pannell Award is given annually to a bookseller whose efforts bring children and books together.

3) WBNA is a reading promotion partner of the Center for the Book in the Library of Congress (§32).

Publications

The Bookwoman is published three times a year; individual chapters publish newsletters as well.

Sources of Support

Membership fees, and publishing companies may contribute as sustaining members.

A Few Other Resources

A number of resources are too important to pass by completely but do not fit neatly into our main list of organizations. Here we note a number of publications and organizations that also belong to the community of the book, a community—as the organization of this section illustrates—that stretches from author and publisher to reader and promoter. Two essential publications from R.R. Bowker should be noted at the outset: *The Bowker Annual of Library and Book Trade Information* and, especially, *LMP/Literary Market Place: The Directory of the American Book Publishing Industry*. *Literary Market Place*, an annual directory of the book trade, includes information about publishers, book clubs, literary agents, book distributors, the book trade, writers' and press associations, desktop publishing, wholesalers, book manufacturers, paper suppliers, binders, and much more. Bowker also publishes *International Literary Market Place*, which provides similar information on a worldwide scale.

Authors and writing. Societies for the study and appreciation of individual authors abound. The current edition of the *Encyclopedia of Associations*, for example, lists more than 110. Mark Twain alone has inspired the formation of 5 U.S. organizations. *Literary Market Place* lists more than 70 writers' organizations under the heading "Book Trade and Allied Associations," including International Black Book Writers, Midwest Travel Writers Association, and Mystery Writers of America. It also lists more than 150 writers' conferences and workshops. Through conventions, publications, and special events, fan clubs in specialized genres, particularly mysteries and science fiction, often are important influences on the market and the genre itself. Detailed information about writers' "colonies and retreats" can be found in *The Guide to Writers Conferences, Seminars, Colonies, Retreats, and Organizations* (Guides Inc., 1990). Several states and many large cities have organizations that support the interests of local writers; examples include the Arizona Authors Association, the Nebraska Writers Guild, the Independent Writers of Chicago, and Washington Independent Writers. *Writer's Northwest Handbook: A Guide to the Northwest's Writing and Publishing Industry* (Media Weavers) is an important regional directory. The monthly *Writer's Digest* (F&W Publications, Inc.) addresses concerns of prospective writers. The quarterly *Visible Language*, published by the Rhode Island School of Design, is "concerned with research and ideas that help define the unique role and properties of written language." Also see main entries for American Society of Journalists and Authors (§14), Associated Writing Programs (§17), Authors League of America, Inc., and Authors Guild, Inc.(§23), PEN American Center (§87), Poets & Writers Inc. (§88), Society of Children's Book Writers and Illustrators (§99) and Teachers & Writers Collaborative (§102).

Publishing. *Publishers Weekly* (New York: Cahners/R.R. Bowker) is the trade magazine of the U.S. book industry. Subtitled "the international news magazine of book publishing," it carries articles that deal with all aspects of the book trade and its advertisements announce publications, advertising plans, printing services, and management services. *Logos: The Professional Journal of the Book World* (Whurr Publishers Ltd.) is a quarterly that "aims to serve the common causes of those engaged in writing, making, selling, and disseminating books and journals throughout the world." *Small Press: The Magazine and Review of Independent Publishing*, published quarterly, is devoted to news of the small press world and reviews of small press books. Other periodicals, such as *Scholarly Publishing* (University of Toronto Press), *Microform Review* (K.G. Saur), and *Publishing Research Quarterly* (Transaction Periodicals Consortium) treat specialized aspects of publishing. Statistics about the book trade can be found in The Book Industry Study Group's *Book Industry Trends* as well as in the section on "Research and Statistics" in *The Bowker Annual.*

Courses for students interested in learning about the book trade are taught at several universities. The Denver Publishing Institute was established in 1976, and summer institutes also are sponsored by Radcliffe College, Stanford University, and others. The Canadian Centre for Studies in Publishing (Simon Fraser University, Burnaby, B.C. V5A 1S6) distributes information about publishing education programs in the U.S. and Canada. *Books and Magazines: A Guide to Publishing and Bookselling Courses in the United States* was published in 1992 by Peterson's Guides with support from the U.S. Information Agency.

Publishing and book development in the Third World is discussed in the occasional *Bellagio Publishing Network Newsletter* (Comparative Education Center, SUNY at Buffalo, Buffalo, N.Y. 14260). Also see the main entries for the Association of American Publishers, Inc. (§19), Association of American University Presses, Inc. (§20), Book Industry Study Group Inc. (§26), COSMEP—The International Association of Independent Publishing (§43), International Publishers Association (§60), Magazine Publishers of America (§66), Multicultural Publishers Exchange (§68), Newspaper Association of America Foundation (§85), PUBWATCH (§92), Small Press Center (§97), and Society for Scholarly Publishing (§98).

Book production and design. There are many groups, in addition to those organizations listed in the main section of this directory, that exchange ideas and sponsor programs about the manufacturing, design, and production of books. Some also produce books. The list includes the Chicago-based American Center for Design, which publishes an annual, the *Design Journal*; Bookbinders Guild of New York; Bookbuilders of Boston; Bookbuilders of Washington; Pacific Center for the Book Arts, Philadelphia Book Clinic; the Pyramid Atlantic Center for Papers, Prints, and Books (Baltimore and Washington); and the University of Iowa Center for the Book. For an extensive listing, see the "Book Trade and Allied Associations" section of *Literary Market Place*. See also the main entries for the American Book Producers Association (§6), American Institute of Graphic Arts (§10), Book Manufacturers' Institute (§27), Bookbuilders West (§28), Center for Book Arts (§31), Chicago Book Clinic (§35), and Guild of Book Workers (§52).

Book arts. Interest in the study and preservation of book arts such as typography, printing, binding, design and graphics, and papermaking has increased during the past decade. Book arts programs are now offered at more than two dozen colleges and universities around the country. Pro Arte Libri (P.O. Box 193394, San Francisco, California 94119) is "an interdisciplinary, international society fostering the cultural values, both artistic and literary, to be found in the making of books." The Minnesota Center for Book Arts (24 North Third Street, Minneapolis, Minnesota 55401; telephone 612-338-3634) preserves and promotes the book arts, concentrating on hand arts and public education. Artists Book Works in Chicago is a local organization founded to preserve and promote the book arts and support book artists. Other regional and local organizations are listed in the preceding section on book production and design. *Book Arts in the USA*, the fifty-three-page summary of a 1990 conference sponsored by the Center for Book Arts, is a valuable description of book arts activity thoughout America. *Bookways: A Quarterly for Book Arts* (Austin) covers news and reviews from the world of contemporary bookmaking and features articles covering all aspects of the book—printing, binding, papermaking, collecting, publishing and more. The issues of *Fine Print* (1975-90) are a rich resource. Also see the main entries for the American Institute of Graphic Arts (§10) and the Center for Book Arts (§31).

Book preservation. Book condition studies conducted in the nation's largest and oldest research libraries have shown that a significant percentage of our printed intellectual heritage (some 25 percent) is deteriorating from the problem of acid degradation of the paper. Most affected are books printed after 1850. A number of organizations have joined forces to call attention to the problem of "brittle books," and conduct cooperative preservation projects to save the most important materials from extinction. Most significant is increasing advocacy for the use of long-lasting, alkaline paper. An *American National Standard for Permanent Paper for Printed Library Materials* was published by the National Information Standards Organization in 1984 (updated in 1992) and most university presses now publish on alkaline paper. The Commission on Preservation and Access (1785 Massachusetts Avenue, N.W., no. 313, Washington, DC 20036; telephone 202-483-7474) is a central, catalytic agency that addresses the entire range of problems related to the preservation of the published and documentary record in all formats and to providing enhanced access to our intellectual and cultural heritage.

In 1988 The New York Public Library established the Center for Paper Permanency, and an independent group, Authors and Publishers in Support of Preservation of the Printed Word, solicits commitments from authors to have their first editions printed on permanent paper. In 1988 Senator Claiborne Pell introduced a joint resolution calling for a "National Policy on Permanent Paper," which was signed into law (P.L. 101-423) in October 1989. Several states have established preservation offices. Publications that describe current preservation activities include the *Abbey Newsletter* (Abbey Publications) and *Conservation Administration News*

(University of Tulsa Libraries). Also see the main entries for the Council on Library Resources (§46), Library of Congress (§64), and the National Information Standards Organization (§81).

Book history. The study of the social and cultural history of books and the effect of print culture on society is a rapidly growing, interdisciplinary field. Important descriptions of the range of topics and resources being explored include *Books and Society in History*, edited by Kenneth E. Carpenter (Bowker, 1983); *Needs and Opportunities in the History of the Book: America, 1639–1876* (American Antiquarian Society, 1987), and Alice D. Schreyer's *The History of Books: A Guide to Selected Resources in the Library of Congress* (Library of Congress, 1987). The Library History Round Table of the American Library Association (ALA) and the History of Reading SIG of the International Reading Association (IRA) are two of the concerned professional groups. The Center for the Study of Southern Culture at the University of Mississippi sponsors an annual "Oxford Conference for the Book." Newly formed organizations include: Society for the History of Authorship, Reading, & Publishing (SHARP), c/o Jonathan Rose, History Department, Drew University, Madison, New Jersey 07940; the Center for the History of Print Culture in Modern America, which is under the joint sponsorship of the University of Wisconsin-Madison and the State Historical Society of Wisconsin; and the Center for the History of the Book, established at Pennsylvania State University at University Park. Other organizations include the Book Trade History Group, University of Leeds (Leeds LS2 9JT, UK); Leipziger Arbeitskreis zur Geschichte des Buchwesens (Leipzig, Germany); Herzog August Bibliothek Wolfenbuttel in Wolfenbuttel, Germany; and the Institut d'Etude du Livre in Paris. Also see the main entries for American Antiquarian Society (§3), American Printing History Association (§13), Bibliographical Society of America (§25), and Center for the Book in the Library of Congress (§32).

Rare books. The Rare Books and Manuscripts Section of the Association of College and Research Libraries (ACRL) of the American Library Association is a major professional force in this field. The ACRL journal, *Rare Books and Manuscripts*, published twice a year, deals with current trends, issues, and publications. Each summer for one week the Rare Book School, organized by Terry Belanger (University of Virginia, 114 Alderman Library, Charlottesville, Virginia 22903-2498) brings experts and students together. *Rare Books 1983-84: Trends, Collections, Sources*, edited by Alice D. Schreyer and published by R.R. Bowker in 1984, is a valuable guide and resource that includes lists of appraisers of books and manuscripts, auctioneers of literary property, and dealers in antiquarian books and manuscripts. Also of value is the pamphlet *Your Old Books* by Peter VanWingen, published by the ACRL. Also see the main entries for the American Antiquarian Society (§3) and Antiquarian Booksellers Association of America (§16).

Book collecting. Book collecting clubs around the country sponsor a wide variety of programs, exhibitions, lectures, and publications on book collecting, rare books, fine printing, the graphic arts, and related topics.

Major clubs include the Grolier Club in New York, founded in 1884; the Club of Odd Volumes in Boston; the Philobiblon Club of Philadelphia; the Rowfant Club in Cleveland; the Caxton Club in Chicago; the Zamorano Club in Los Angeles; the Book Club of California and the Roxburghe Club in San Francisco; the Baltimore Bibliophiles; the Pittsburgh Bibliophiles; and the Book Club of Texas. Two volumes edited by Jean Peters, *Book Collecting: A Modern Guide* (Bowker, 1977) and *Collectible Books: Some New Paths* (Bowker, 1979), provide a comprehensive introduction to book collecting.

Bookselling. *Publishers Weekly* contains much of interest, and *American Bookseller* (American Booksellers Association) is the basic trade magazine. The *American Book Trade Directory* (Bowker) lists bookstores and book wholesalers. Regional book trade organizations and associations exist in most areas. Many parts of *Literary Market Place* are relevant to the bookselling business as well as to publishing. The antiquarian and rare book trade relies on *AB/Bookman's Weekly* (Clifton, New Jersey), a valuable resource that also carries news about current happenings throughout the book world. Also see main entries for the African American Publishers and Booksellers Association (§2), American Booksellers Association (§7), American Whole Booksellers Association (§15), Antiquarian Booksellers Association of America (§16), Association of Booksellers for Children (§21), Christian Booksellers Association (§40), and National Association of College Stores (§70).

Libraries. *Library Journal* (Bowker), *American Libraries* (American Library Association), *Wilson Library Bulletin* (H.W. Wilson Company), *Special Libraries* (Special Libraries Association), and the *School Library Journal* (Bowker) are principal sources of news and information. *Alexandria: The Journal of National & International Library and Information Issues* (Ashgate Publishing/The British Library) is concerned with both policy and practice. In addition, associations, university departments, and professional publishers produce a great number of journals and newsletters for particular areas of librarianship. The *American Library Directory* provides information about individual public, academic, government, and special libraries in the United States and valuable supplementary information. The *Bowker Annual of Library and Book Trade Information* includes sections on library legislation, funding, and grants, as well as a calendar of important upcoming events and a directory of library organizations. Also see the main entries for the American Library Association (§12), Association of Research Libraries (§22), Council on Library Resources, Inc. (§46), Friends of Libraries U.S.A. (§49), International Federation of Library Associations & Institutions (§59), Library of Congress (§64), and Special Libraries Association (§100).

Book reviewing. Only a small percentage of the fifty thousand or so books published each year in the United States are reviewed—or receive any kind of published notice. The *New York Times Book Review* is this country's leading general book review, but book review sections in newspapers seem to become fewer each year. The *New York Review of*

Books, and the *Times Literary Supplement* provide valuable and often opinionated reviews. The "Book Reviews, Exhibits, Clubs and Lists" section of *Literary Market Place* lists book review syndicates, journals, and indexes, including a vast array of specialized scholarly and professional journals and services. *AudioFile* (P.O. Box 109, Portland, ME 04112-0109, telephone 207-774-7563) is a monthly newsletter of reviews of audio books.

Book discussion groups. There is a revival of informal book discussion groups throughout America. Many are sponsored, or at least hosted, by bookstores or libraries, but other organizations also are involved, including the National Issues Forum (100 Commons Road, Dayton, Ohio 45459-2777). The "Let's Talk about It" project of the National Endowment for the Humanities and American Library Association stimulates such discussions, as does the Great Books Foundation (§50) for works of great literature and the Chautauqua Literary and Scientific Circle (§34). Information is also available from the Study Circle Resources Center, P.O. Box 203, 697A Pomfret Road, Pomfret, Connecticut 06258.

Book awards. Awards are an increasingly popular means of recognizing achievement in the book world. Most of the awards honor authors, but others mark distinction in bookmaking and in the book professions. Information about awards can be found in *Literary Market Place, The Bowker Annual of Library and Book Trade Information,* and in *Children's Books: Awards & Prizes: 1992* (Children's Book Council, Inc.). The National Book Critics Circle, (c/o Jack Miles, 3568 East Mountain View Avenue, Pasadena, California 91107), a national professional nonprofit association of book critics and book review editors, annually presents awards in biography, criticism, fiction, nonfiction, and poetry. Three state centers for the book (Colorado, Minnesota, Oklahoma) sponsor awards programs. Also see the main entry for the National Book Foundation (§71) and PEN American Center (§86).

Book fairs, festivals, and exhibits. Major international book fairs such as the annual fairs in Frankfurt, Bologna, London, and Jerusalem are listed in *Literary Market Place*'s section, "Calendar of Book Trade & Promotional Events." Book fairs are growing in popularity in the United States. *Fanfare for Words: Bookfairs and Book Festivals in North America* (Library of Congress, 1991) provides an extensive list of bookfairs. Examples include New York Is Book Country, the Miami Book Fair International, the Oklahoma Cowboy Poetry Gathering, and Sacramento Reads: A Celebration of Words. Children's book fairs are important, too. Library Theatre (Bethesda, Maryland) uses musical theater to bring books to life and motivate children to read. School Book Fairs, Inc. (Worthington, Ohio), sponsors Kids Are Authors, an annual event to honor young authors. WaldenEd, a book fair company, is a subsidiary of Waldenbooks. Texas School Book Fairs is a division of Scholastic Book Fairs, Inc. Also see the main entry for Children's Literacy Initiative (§37).

Literacy and reading promotion initiatives. Since the publication in 1983 of *A Nation at Risk,* the widely publicized report of the National Commission on Excellence in Education, there has been a dramatic increase in the number and kind of projects to combat illiteracy and motivate reading. The private sector, in particular, has become increasingly committed to aiding education, literacy, and reading promotion. This directory, in the main entries listed below, mentions many of the projects, both private and governmental. Additional examples include Pizza Hut's BOOK IT!, a national reading incentive program in elementary schools; Time Warner's "Time to Read" literacy program; Coors' "Literacy, Pass It On" project; 7-Eleven's "People Who Read Achieve" project; GTE Sylvania's "America's Official Reading Time" program; and Six Flags Theme Parks' "Read to Succeed" program. Also see the main entries for the American Library Association (§12), Association for Community-Based Education (§18), Barbara Bush Foundation for Family Literacy (§24), Cartoonists Across America (§29), Center for the Book in the Library of Congress (§32), Contact Literacy Center (§41, Graphic Arts Literacy Alliance (§50, Institute for Study of Adult Literacy (§55), Literacy Volunteers of America (§65), National Center for Family Literacy (§72), National Center on Adult Literacy (§73), National Coalition for Literacy (§75), National Institute for Literacy (§82), Newspaper Association of America Foundation (§85), Project Learning U.S. (§90), Push Literacy Action Now (§93), Reading Is Fundamental, Inc. (§94), Reading Reform Foundation (§96), and U.S. Department of Education (§104). It should be noted that the Business Council for Effective Literacy (BCEL), established in 1983, closed its doors on June 30, 1993.

Book culture promotion. Books, reading, and literacy promotion are active functions of government in most countries outside the United States. The Canadian Organization for the Development of Education is a Canadian nongovernmental, nonprofit organization that supports education and literacy work in the Third World through its well- known book shipping/book donation program. Since 1988, the National Library of Canada has sponsored "Read Up on It/Lisez sur le Sujet" to promote Canadian books and reading. In Great Britain, the British Council actively supports British book culture and the Book Trust promotes books and reading, particularly for young people through the Children's Book Foundation. The Centre for the Book in the British Library was established in 1990 "to promote the significance of the book, in all its forms, as a vital part of the cultural, commercial and scientific life of the country, past and present." Other similar organizations include Australia's National Book Council, located in Carlton; the New Zealand Council, in Wellington; the Deutsche Lesegesellschaft, in Mainz, Germany; and the Fundacion Germain Sanchez Ruiperez, in Salamanca, Spain. Unesco (Books and Copyright Division, 7, Place de Fontenoy, 75700 Paris) promotes book development, and the strengthening of national infrastructures for book production and distribution. It emphasizes technical assistance, publishes manuals for the training of publishers, booksellers, and writers, and works in cooperation with regional centers in Africa, Asia, and Latin America. Unesco also promotes reading, particularly among children, young adults, and the newly literate.

Index

Information in "Is There a Community of the Book?" and "A Few Other Resources" is indexed to page numbers (p.), whereas information in the main body of organizations is indexed to section numbers (§). Section numbers in **boldface** indicate an entry devoted to that organization.

In addition to a few publications indexed here, almost every organization in the main list publishes a newsletter, which has been noted in the entry for that organization.

147